THE
SOCIAL
RESPONSIBILITY
OF
CHRISTIANS

THE KNUBEL-MILLER LECTURES—1960

The
Social
Responsibility
of
Christians

By

A. D. Mattson

BOARD OF PUBLICATION
OF THE UNITED LUTHERAN CHURCH IN AMERICA
PHILADELPHIA

PREFACE

The theme assigned for the Knubel-Miller Lectures for 1960 is "The Social Responsibility of Christians." In 1943 I published a book titled *Christian Social Consciousness* and some of the material in the present series of lectures will be a repetition of some of the things said in that book. However, the approach will be quite different. The present lectures will be more concerned with the theological postulates of a social ethics than the earlier volume, and with the various types of biblical religion.

Theological liberalism and a social ethical emphasis are not synonymous. I am grateful for many insights which liberalism has contributed to my theological development, but I am not a liberal. I hope it will be quickly apparent that I do not belong to a fundamentalist camp, either. Likewise, I have always had—and still hold—many reservations with respect to the type of theology which developed after the close of the First World War, and is now the fashion in many circles. There is a classical Christian tradition—we might say an orthodox tradition—and in this tradition I feel most at home. Modern scholarship has made significant contributions to a more adequate understanding of that tradition, but there is a main channel; and in that stream I trust that the theological presuppositions of these lectures will be found.

Many, in both orthodox and liberal traditions, have become alarmed at the lack of an ethical emphasis in some theological circles during the last quarter of a century. Where the ethical has been emphasized at all, it often has been ethics without content. In this series of lectures I shall try to point out some of the attitudes in modern theology which tend to destroy its ethical relevance. The ethical impact of the Christian faith upon society will, of course, be the primary consideration.

I am deeply indebted and grateful to Walter Rauschenbusch for his influence upon my thinking during the time I was a college and seminary student. The impact of his works has been an inspiration through the years. I am also mindful of the influence of Nathan Soderblom, which will be apparent in these lectures. Both of these giants, at the time they were at the height of their prestige, did much to develop a sense of social responsibility in the young student, and the years have not dimmed their significance.

A. D. Mattson

TABLE OF CONTENTS

ix

1

THE MEANING OF
SOCIAL RESPONSIBILITY

The Christian Faith Involves an Ethic

Back in 1930, Alfred E. Garvie reacted negatively to the type of theological development which was taking place on the Continent, and the efforts which were being made to "make it the fashion of the hour" in England, also. He said "there is an almost Manichaean, Gnostic dualism in this theology between the relative and the absolute, world and God, God's imminence and God's transcendence. Man's sin, great and grievous as it is, has not so corrupted the world that it has ceased to be the world God made, preserves, and rules, in which He still is and works."[1] Garvie sensed what was taking place in the postwar theological climate, and many who have followed the theological developments of the last thirty years have often been alarmed at the progress of the trend which Garvie so clearly saw. Paul Holmer, in a recent issue of the *Christian Century*, expresses his apprehension when he says that "much of recent theology—neo-orthodoxy if you will—cuts the nerve of ethical endeavor."[2] The position is often emphasized that the exigencies of the historical situation make it impossible to apply the Christian

---

[1] Alfred E. Garvie, *The Christian Ideal for Human Society* (West Rindge, N.H.: Richard R. Smith, Inc., 1930), p. 467.
[2] Paul Holmer, "Modern Theology, Another Evasion?" *Christian Century* (Chicago), January 22, 1958, p. 103.

ideal. There is a truth involved in this attitude which must be recognized, but we must never allow a compromising position to become the ideal. After all, it is not the historical situation which is determinative for the Christian, it is the will of God. We need to guard against committing idolatry by making the historical situation determinative. If the historical situation is to be determinative, then it is no longer God who is sovereign and, like the situation in Marxian communism, historical forces become God. In the last analysis, based on such a position, ethics loses its religious basis.

Christian social responsibility is ethical responsibility. A kind of Gnostic dualism which emphasizes justification but neglects to stress the "birth of a new self who finds his place in the world of existence by devotion to the will of God,"[3] will not be the classical Christian faith, and it will not be the answer which the world seeks and needs.

The biblical tradition places the ethical concern in the nature of God himself. The "wisdom" literature of the Old Testament is a pregnant example. The word wisdom meant, primarily, "moral principle." Wisdom was virtually the equivalent of goodness. It was spiritual insight, a true discrimination of values, and an understanding of what is most worthful. Wisdom had its roots in religion, so to be wise meant to estimate the values of life from God's standpoint. For the wise man, God was at the center of life and governed thought, word, and deed.[4] In Proverbs 8:22 ff., wisdom is spoken of as the first creation of God, which is now present among men as the mouthpiece and representative of God. Wisdom is the impersonation of a moral quality. The ethical quality of wisdom is also emphasized in Ecclesiasticus, where it is identified with the "law that Moses commanded."[5]

[3] Carl F. H. Henry, *Christian Personal Ethics* (Michigan: William B. Eerdman's Publishing Company, 1957), p. 394.
[4] Prov. 1:7.
[5] Ecclus. 24:3 ff.

In Wisdom of Solomon 7:22 ff., wisdom is the "artificer of all things" and "the brightness (effulgence) of the everlasting light and an unstained mirror of the power of God," and it penetrates and permeates all things.

In the works of Philo, the Logos idea is the equivalent of wisdom. In the fourth Gospel, Jesus is identified with the Logos;[6] and in the Letter to the Hebrews Jesus is spoken of as "the effulgence of his (God's) glory."[7]

Similar to the fourth Gospel and the Letter to the Hebrews are the Epistles of Paul, when they apply terms to Jesus which had originally been applied to wisdom. In fact, Paul calls Jesus "the wisdom of God"[8] and then he adds he was made "unto us wisdom from God, and righteousness and sanctification, and redemption. . . ."[9] He says in Christ "are all the treasures of wisdom and knowledge hidden."[10] As wisdom was the first creation of God, so also is Christ "the firstborn of all creation."[11]

It is evident that the role which wisdom played in the Old Testament and in the Apocrypha is transferred to Jesus in the New Testament. Jesus was the manifestation of the wisdom or the "moral principle" of God. He was the revelation of perfect goodness. Whatever else the doctrine of the divinity of Christ means, it does mean that Jesus revealed God in the goodness and the moral quality of his character. Jesus Christ is the "image" of God.[12] The divine is manifest in the moral perfection of the life of Jesus, and thus the ethical is bound up with the very being of God himself. The essence of the moral is a unity, and it is identical, though not in degree, for both God and man.

[6] John 1.
[7] Heb. 1:3.
[8] I Cor. 1:24.
[9] I Cor. 1:30.
[10] Col. 2:3.
[11] Col. 1:15.
[12] Col. 1:15.

Social Ethics and the New Testament

It was Jesus himself who said, "Truly, I say to you, as you did it to one of the least of these my brethren, you did it to me."[13] This does not mean that Christ is troubled from a distance by the needs of our fellow men, but that love's identity and unity places our human woes upon him. Saul, when he journeyed to Damascus to persecute the Christians there, heard Christ say, ". . . why persecutest thou me?"[14] Christ, as Paul conceived it, identified himself with these persecuted men and women. "In all their affliction he was afflicted. . . ."[15] Again, the Christian faith places a social concern in the nature of God himself.

As "God is love" so also is the Christian life one that is lived in love to God and the neighbor. Love to God and love of fellow man belong together. According to the First Epistle of John, "If any one says, 'I love God,' and hates his brother, he is a liar; for he who does not love his brother whom he has seen, cannot love God whom he has not seen."[16] The ground of the Christian ethic is not to be found in any kind of hedonism, utilitarianism, eudaemonism, or in that which makes for good human relations, but in the love and will of God. This love cannot be separated from the love of fellow man for love is a unity. Any such separation is an illusion. A lack of ethical love separates man from the life which is in fellowship with God. Failure to love our neighbor cancels our love to God because God is love. If God's nature is love, then we must love in order to love God.

Anders Nygren has had considerable trouble in dealing with the concept of love in relation to God, as the concept is difficult to fit into his theory. Instead of speaking, as Jesus did, about love to God, he feels that faith is the term to use

---

13 Matt. 25:40.   14 Acts 22:7.
15 Isa. 63:9.
16 I John 4:20.

when we speak about man's relationship to God.[17] He holds that the concept involved in "agape" in the Johannine writings is fluctuating and that the distinction between "motivated" and "unmotivated" love is not clearly maintained.[18] Precisely so. The facts do not fit the theory. "Agape" does not always mean "unmotivated love" as Nygren maintains it should, and he makes the mistake of overlooking the flexibility in the use of words. He rejects emphatically the idea of "loving God in our neighbor."[19] He rightly emphasizes that there are differences between man's love of God and man's love of fellow man, but he fails to see that Christian love is a unity which includes both God and man as the author of I John emphasizes. Here again the Christian finds himself faced with a social responsibility which proceeds out of the very nature of the Christian life and experience. If we fail to assert the unity of love, which I John emphasizes, our theology and religion may simply become an escape from social responsibility, and it is to be noted that there is very little emphasis on social responsibility where this unity is not maintained.

Religion and morality belong together in the New Testament. Jesus would not allow what were considered to be religious observances to negate the manifestation of love to fellow man.[20] A classical example is found in Mark 7:9-13, R.S.V. Jesus said to the Pharisees: "You have a fine way of rejecting the commandment of God, in order to keep your tradition! For Moses said, 'Honor your father and your mother'; and, 'He who speaks evil of father or mother, let him surely die'; but you say, 'If a man tells his father or his mother, What you would have gained from me is Corban' (that is, given to God) —then you no longer permit him to

---

[17] Anders Nygren, *Agape and Eros* (Stockholm: Svenska Kyrkans Diakonis-tyrelses Bokforlag, 1930), p. 94.
[18] *Ibid.*, p. 118.   [19] *Ibid.*, p. 70.
[20] Mark 3:1-6.

do anything for his father or mother, thus making void the word of God through your tradition which you hand on. And many such things you do." Jesus here, in a very radical way, has abolished any separation between religion and morality. Religion and morality are not identical, and we cannot confine religion to the ethical, but they are inseparably united in the Christian faith.

In the last sentence of the first part of the *Small Catechism,* Luther emphasizes this relationship when he says, "We should therefore love him, trust him, and cheerfully do what he has commanded." Luther's explanation of the First Article emphasizes the same idea when he says, "For all of this I am bound to thank, praise, serve, and obey him." In his explanation of the Second Petition he says that faith in the Word of God leads to "a godly life here on earth." Love to God becomes an empty form if it does not manifest itself in love to neighbor. This relationship is so intimate that the author of I John could say, "this is the love of God, that we keep his commandments."[21]

A seldom quoted passage from scripture, which describes a sense of social consciousness and responsibility, is a prayer from the primitive church. The social implications of this prayer are so often overlooked that we shall quote it in its entirety. Peter and John had been released from prison, and when they returned to the company of their fellow believers this prayer was offered:

> "Sovereign Lord, who didst make the heaven and the earth and the sea and everything in them, who by the mouth of our father David, thy servant, didst say by the Holy Spirit,
> 'Why did the Gentiles rage,
> and the peoples imagine vain things?

---

[21] I John 5:3.

The kings of the earth set themselves in array,
and the rulers were gathered together,
Against the Lord and against his Anointed'—
for truly in this city there were gathered together against
thy holy servant Jesus, whom thou didst anoint, both
Herod and Pontius Pilate, with the Gentiles and the
peoples of Israel, to do whatever thy hand and thy
plan had predestined to take place. And now, Lord, look
upon their threats, and grant to thy servants to speak
thy word with all boldness, while thou stretchest out
thy hand to heal, and signs and wonders are performed
through the name of thy Holy servant Jesus."[22]

The members of this primitive church knew it was imperative for them to take a stand with respect to the political
and cultural situation in which they found themselves. A
union of Roman political authority and vested religious
interests had crucified Jesus. Political forces of the time were
powers opposed to God and his will. Herod and Pontius
Pilate were political instruments opposed to God. Government may be an instrument in the service of God or it may
be a power which is opposed to God, and this fact was very
clear to this primitive Christian community. Its members
were conscious of the responsibility to take a position in
relation to the political forces which surrounded them. This
was their Christian social responsibility.

The apostle Paul has sometimes been interpreted in a
manner leaving little room for any dynamic for a sense of
social responsibility; but it was Paul who wrote "God was in
Christ reconciling the *world* to himself," and has committed
to us the ministry of reconciliation.[23] Here Paul sees the
Christian gospel in terms of a reconciliation of the world to

[22] Acts 4:24-30.
[23] II Cor. 5:19.

God, and this involves a sense of social responsibility. The Christian faith, in Paul's conception, was more than a matter of individual salvation, or ecstatic feeling, or a rejoicing in the hope of a heaven after death. Paul's hope involved the reconciliation of the world to God.

The Christian sense of responsibility for the social order is also found in the last book of the Bible—a book where we might least expect to find it. The holy city, or the new Jerusalem, is a city that comes down to earth from out of heaven. It is not heaven itself.[24] The millennial hope in the Book of Revelation is a social hope which emphasizes the Christian's concern with the social order. When Revelation was written, Rome was the mistress of the world and the church was feeble and persecuted. The millennial hope involves that the roles will ultimately be reversed. God's people will see a fruition of their labor and suffering even in this world. This hope is an inspiration for social welfare and social justice. God has not abandoned his world or the realm of history. As long as the temporal lasts, evil may again manifest itself. The author of Revelation takes sin very seriously, but the Christian still maintains his hope for the social order and history.[25] We have no outline of history in advance, but we do have a hope which includes history because this is God's world.

The passage in the New Testament which emphasizes social responsibility, and which is used more often than any other, is the third petition of the Lord's Prayer. From its primitive days, and to the present time, the church and Christians have prayed:

> Thy kingdom come,
> Thy will be done,
> *On earth* as it is in heaven.

[24] Rev. 21:1-2.   [25] Rev. 20.

We pray that God's will may be done *on earth* and thus assert a sense of responsibility for the social order. Someone has said that the first casualty in prayer is the one who really prays; and we cannot really pray the third petition of the Lord's Prayer unless we have a sense of social responsibility. God desires that his will be done in the things of earth, and the Christian cannot be indifferent to them if he is to be faithful to the object of his faith. And as Christians we cannot wait, for God's will does not wait.

The New Testament is replete with a sense of social responsibility. As we become aware of this fact, the meaning of our social responsibility becomes clear. The relation of the Christian to God involves more than a dual relationship. God and the individual soul are involved, but our relationship to God involves a trinity: God, the individual soul, and our neighbor. As our relationship to our neighbor enters the picture, we find ourselves in the realm of the social and social responsibility. As the consciousness of our relationship to God develops, the sense of solidarity with our fellow men increases. The Christian is a sinner who stands in need of God's forgiving grace, but justification is not something which is unrelated to the rest of life or social responsibility. Luther put it this way: ". . . for where there is forgiveness of sins, there are also life and salvation."[26] The forgiven sinner lives in an atmosphere which becomes meaningful for life. The forgiven sinner is called to a life of service, and God will only be served as we recognize our God-given responsibilities to our fellow men. There is no bypass to God, from the point of view of Christian faith, which ignores our relationship to our neighbor. There are attitudes connected with the worship life of the church which give the blasphemous impression of a kind of Divine egocentricity on the part of God. Worship of God without ethical emphasis and

[26] *Small Catechism.*

devotion is an insult to him who finds his highest honor in serving. Luther said it is the glory of God that he is a blessing to us.[27]

Social Welfare

Christian social responsibility is an integral factor in the Christian faith and life, and it manifests itself in two directions. In the first place, it is directed to minister to the physical and temporal needs of our fellow men. Social missions and inner missions are terms well known in the history of the church. The Bible is full of this type of ministry—from cover to cover. The healing ministry of Jesus and Paul's collection for the poor are well-known examples. Social service is a Christian obligation and Christians universally have recognized it as such. When certain groups in the church are confronted with the criticism that they are quietistic, by way of defense they often will point to the charitable institutions they have established and maintained. Hospitals, orphan homes, homes for the aged, homes for epileptics, and many similar institutions, are manifestations of a faith which energizes in love, and there would be something lacking in a Christianity unconcerned with the human needs to which such institutions minister. The Christian's concern for his neighbor will and should manifest itself in caring for the indigent.

The Spiritual and the Material

In rendering service as described above, the Christian does not set up an antithesis between spiritual and material realms. Such an attitude is well illustrated by Dr. Gibson,

[27] *Gloria eius est, quod beneficus in nos est* as reported in *Lectures on Romans* from *D. Martin Luthers Werke* Kritische Gesamtausgabe (Weimar, 1883-   ). Hereafter referred to as *WA*.

the Bishop of London, to whom the religious care of plantations and slaves in America had been entrusted. In 1727 he wrote: "The freedom which Christianity gives is a freedom from the bondage of sin and Satan and from the dominion of man's lusts and passions and inordinate desires. . . ." but, as to slavery, ". . . it makes no manner of change in it." The Lutheran Synod of South Carolina, in 1846, heard its president say, "Lutherans having slaves should exercise their right as masters to bring them to attend divine worship in the churches where they hold their membership; and if such slaves desire to enter into church relations, let them be advised to unite with the churches where their owners enkindle their devotions at the altars of God." Slaves had souls that could be made eternally happy, but often there was no concern about the temporal slavery of these people.

The Christian does not minister in the form of material blessings in order to bring a spiritual blessing to the recipient. The Good Samaritan ministered to the physical needs of the man who had fallen into the hands of robbers on the road between Jerusalem and Jericho. There is nothing in the parable that indicates he was concerned about an Evangelistic message before he left him at the inn. Here was need, and that need was met; and the Good Samaritan was commended by the Lord for his act. The material and the spiritual are not different categories. The spiritual may manifest itself through the material things of life. The word "spiritual" may be used to describe the incorporeal, but it does not mean a lack of interest in the material. Paul exhorts his readers to present their material bodies as a spiritual worship.[28] The spiritual involves having a nature in which spirit predominates, or it is the human spirit led and guided by the Spirit of God.

Material things may be used for spiritual service. Moses

[28] Rom. 12:1.

rendered a spiritual service when he delivered his people from their Egyptian bondage. Moses was concerned about developing a right relation to God on the part of his people, but when he delivered them from their slavery he acted because they needed to be freed. Jesus "did not heal in order to commend himself or to overcome opposition or prejudice, for some of his miracles resulted in stirring up opposition and he knew they would so result. He did not heal to attract a crowd, for, as in Mark 8:30, he sometimes '. . . charged them that they tell no man. . . .' He does not seem, even, to be concerned with making use of the evangelistic opportunity to preach to those he healed. His ministry of healing was just not done casually, as if secondary and unimportant. He put forth both physical and spiritual energy to heal men. He refused to perform works of healing as signs. He is not described anywhere in the Synoptic Gospels as using his cures as texts for sermons."[29] This statement is by the Christian Medical Association of India, and it indicates the proper perspective on the Christian attitude toward temporal needs. To urge people to establish hospitals so that we may get a chance to preach to their sick is hardly an honest motive. To be sure, the Christian desires to share the whole Christ with his fellow men; but when we minister to the sick we minister because they are ill, and not for some other reason. We care for the orphan because he is an orphan and for no other reason. Wherever there is need, we desire to minister because there is need. Any other motive violates the fundamental nature of Christian love.

A labor leader once asked me if my interest in the labor movement was prompted by the desire to get labor people to join the church organization. My answer was, in effect, "I certainly am interested in seeing labor people share in

[29] Seward Hiltner, *Religion and Health* (New York: The Macmillan Company, 1943), p. 42.

the blessings of the church, but I am interested in seeing justice done to labor even if I find it impossible to induce them to affiliate with the church. Christian love functions in the presence of need simply because there is need." This point of view is of more than academic interest, as is well illustrated by an article which appeared in a southern labor newspaper a few years ago. It speaks of the "tent preacher" who appears "from distant places with a full knowledge of all our wickedness and of all our spiritual needs, and comes in raving about our spiritual and moral truancy, and carries on night after night, crying himself prostrate about our spiritual and moral delinquency, and tells us of the great things we are to inherit if we follow his teachings—after we are dead. . . .

"It is amazing that ministers are so deeply concerned that we workers shall miss none of those golden blessings promised us after we are dead, but concern themselves so little with the tribulations of millions of Americans who struggle homelessly and hopelessly through this vast wilderness of unemployment, beridden of hunger and sickness of body and soul, seeking friends and relief from this stifling tragedy, but finding only people who wish to save our souls.

"Our Bible teaches that Jesus Christ not only loved the soul of mankind but their body as well. He not only healed the festered spirit of men, but usually their body first. The sick he made well, the hungry he fed—and then he preached, which inspires us to ask, can a preacher love our wicked soul so profoundly without having some affection for our body? Can a sick soul be healed as quickly and efficiently in a hungry, pain-racked body as in a body well and comfortable?

"We read, we listen, and we wonder. 'Beware of false prophets, who come to you in sheep's clothing, but inwardly are ravening wolves.'[30]" Such is labor's grievance.

[30] Matt. 7:15.

Social Action

The Christian is interested in serving his fellow man simply because there is need for such service, and this disposition encompasses both physical and spiritual needs. It means caring for the helpless and the indigent, but there is another direction in which Christian social responsibility manifests itself. The Christian is also concerned about the conditions which produce the need for charity. The Good Samaritan performed a Christian service when he came to the man who had fallen among robbers ". . . and bound up his wounds, pouring on them oil and wine; and he set him on his own beast, and brought him to an inn, and took care of him."[31] The Christian has an added interest in such a situation from the point of view of his social responsibility. The Christian is also concerned about making the road between Jerusalem and Jericho safe, so that men may travel that road without falling into the hands of robbers. Such manifestation of Christian love may not be as dramatic or sentimental as the former, but it is ofttimes more effective. The Christian is interested in rescuing the drunkard, but he should also be interested in the situations in the structure of society which produce drunkards. The average rescue mission performs a real Christian service in caring for the indigent, but the Christian should also be interested in doing something about the slum areas of our large cities, which produce many of the dregs of society with which the Rescue Mission deals. It is a Christian service to minister to the victims of flood waters, but it is likewise a Christian obligation to seek the prevention of floods. Christianity is concerned about the cure of the victims of social maladjustments, but also with preventing people from becoming victims.

[31] Luke 10:34.

Recently a church member was trying to justify the concern of her church for the laboring man by pointing out that an organization in the church had distributed baskets of food to the needy at Thanksgiving and Christmas. To be sure, it is an act of Christian love to feed the hungry, but it is a more significant attitude to be concerned about working conditions which bring about such need for food. Various groups and organizations connected with the church in Germany have made a significant effort to establish friendly relationships with the industrial workers, particularly since the end of the Second World War. A very significant aspect of this approach has been a concern for justice for the worker as against mere charity. Charity is a Chrstian virtue but so, also, is justice. The giving of alms where there is need is not to be depreciated as a social responsibility for the Christian, but there must also be a concern for situations which produce the need for alms. We must care for the aged who cannot care for themselves. This may be done through building and maintaining homes for the aged, but it can also be done by an adequate social security program; and the latter is as involved in the Christian attitude as the former. The promotion of an effective social security program may be a much more effective approach to the problems of the aged than the establishment of homes for these people. There always will be a need for charity and there always will be people who cannot take care of themselves, but Christian social responsibility implies a concern for the elimination of those things in the structure of society which produce indigent people. This is the distinction between "welfare" and "social action." Both are necessary and both are involved in Christian social responsibility. It is in the realm of social action that the church and Christian too often have failed to recognize their social responsibility. It is at this point that an awakening must take place if the church is going to meet the crisis of our age in a realistic fashion. As men seek for meaning and direction for life, they will not find it in the ministry of the church unless the church comes to grips with the problems involved in social action. The old taunt song about "pie in the sky" and the Marxian challenge about religion being the opiate of the people may involve historical reflections which may cause serious soul-searching on the part of Christians and the church. Social responsibility involves a sense of responsibility for the character of society. Holding out the hope of heavenly bliss cannot be a substitute for such things as adequate housing, decent wages, security for old age, and an opportunity to educate the young.

The Realm of Culture

We have already stated that the Christian faith involves God, the individual soul, and our fellow men. Any attempt to distinguish between "individual" and "social ethics" soon reveals that any such line of demarcation becomes rather tenuous. However, there is a realm of experience which is relatively private in nature. Our friendships, love, marriage, and our interior hopes and worries are peculiarly our own individual experiences. In addition to this rather private aspect of human experience, there is another realm. It has to do with the whole field of history, work, industry, government, and society in general. It is the realm of culture or civilization. H. Richard Niebuhr has well defined this realm when he says: "Culture is the 'artificial secondary environment' which man superimposes on the natural. It comprises language, habits, ideas, beliefs, customs, social organization, inherited articrafts, technical processes, and values. This 'social heritage,' this 'reality sui generis,' which the New Testament writers frequently had in mind when they spoke of 'the world,' which is represented in many forms but to which Christians like other men are inevitably subject, is what we mean when we speak of culture."[32] Our religion is not excluded from this realm. God will, in the long run, have to be recognized as the Lord of all of life or we shall fail to recognize him as the Lord of those areas to which we have attempted to confine his activities. A Catholic theologian in Germany has said that Hitler was concerned to confine the studies of theological students to areas which dealt with liturgies and "pure theology" (which meant theology detached from culture). Neither the Fascists nor the Communists have ever been particularly concerned with such theological disciplines. They have, however, been tremendously concerned with religion at the point where it touches the realm of culture. The martyrs and the persecuted heroes of the faith, in our age and in many other ages, have experienced the wrath of the demonic forces of life when they have come to grips with the cultural aspects of their environment. The experience of the church in modern times makes it clear that we cannot confine religion to the sacristy or to a theological "ivory tower." It will, in the long run, be increasingly difficult to keep it in these limited areas unless we come to grips with the social problem. The kind of religion which is confined to the four walls of the sanctuary and to the so-called realm of the "inner life" does not have the answer that our generation seeks and needs. The Christian life is not lived in a vacuum, but in a concrete historical situation with which it is involved. The Christian must seek to live his life as a Christian in the historical context in which he finds himself, or his faith will lack vitality. Even the pillar saint cannot sever various connections with the social order without perishing.

The realm of history, culture, and civilization is involved

[32] Helmut Richard Niebuhr, *Christ and Culture* (New York: Harper and Brothers, 1951), p. 32.

in Christian experience, and when we recognize this fact we soon discover that there are social situations which transcend the individual will and which cannot be dealt with from the point of view of the individual will. There are problems which are specifically social in character. There are problems which can be solved by the will of the individual. But there are also problems which can be solved only as the patterns and forms of society are altered. Among the latter are: war, the relations between capital and labor, poverty, the concentration of wealth, child labor, racial relations, crime, amusements, population problems, and the care of dependent classes. These problems involve situations which are not subject to the immediate will of the individual. For example, an individual may will not to strike his neighbor, and thus prevent such action from taking place. However, when war comes, no amount of willing on the part of the individual will prevent the inflicting of suffering on people. In war, men participate in a situation which is not amenable to their immediate wills. The individual has little to say about the declaration of war, or his participation in it. It is difficult to imagine applying the spirit of Christ to our enemies in a war situation. The problem can never be solved on the basis of individual attitudes. It must be faced as a social problem, and the only solution is to be found in the abolition of the war system as an instrument of the policy of nations. The United Nations organization was established for the purpose of accomplishing this and other objectives. As a Christian, I feel it to be my obligation to support this effort to solve this great social problem in a social way. I hate war but, apart from efforts of this kind, I am helpless to cope with the problem.

An individual may be perfectly honest in his dealing with banks. He may will that depositors in a bank shall not lose their savings, but to insure this fact will require something more than is involved in his individual willing. The depression of the 1930 decade taught us it was necessary to establish new government regulations for banks if people were to be protected; and it is a Christian obligation to be concerned that such protection be provided.

Anyone who has even elementary knowledge of the problems involved in the relations of capital and labor must realize that a solution must be sought in a manner quite different from the manner in which individual problems are solved. Experience has taught us that laws and organization are necessary to cope with the problems involved. Without organization and a social approach the individual worker is ofttimes helpless.

Child labor is another example of a problem which cannot be left for its solution to the individual will. History tells us that the abuse of children in the early days of our modern industrial development was stopped only through social legislation.

One of the best examples of the manner in which social situations effect Christian ethical conduct is found in the economic realm. As Christians, we participate in an economic order. In the measure that such a system is unchristian, we are not, to that extent, living the Christian life; and the only remedy for such a situation is to create a system where it is possible to practice more adequately that which is ethical from the Christian point of view. In other words, the problem can only be solved as a social matter. The isolated individual is helpless to do anything about it. For example, a Christian employer may try, as an individual, to deal fairly with the employees; and the result of such an attitude may be bankruptcy for him because of competition with other employers who are not benevolent in their attitudes to their employees. This problem must be solved as a social problem if it is to be solved at all. There are many businessmen who have come to the conclusion that it is impossible to operate a single, isolated business on Christian principles.

The difference between approaching a problem and its solution from an individual and a social point of view can be illustrated by imagining a city which has no water to meet the needs of its inhabitants. Every Christian would recognize that it is a Christian duty to give a thirsty fellow man a drink of water. The situation might be met in two ways. A pail of water might be brought from some source of supply. The person desiring to minister to the needs of the people might visit as many individuals as possible with a pail and cup, and thus provide as many as possible with water. Another way to meet the situation would be to employ engineers to build a pipeline, and thus bring a supply of water into the city. The latter would certainly be the better way to solve the problem, and it need be no less Christian in spirit than the former. Until we understand that there are situations and problems which can only be approached from a social point of view, we shall never understand the full implications of Christian social responsibility.

A sense of social responsibility involves recognition of the fact that there are certain patterns or forms of society in which the Christian life cannot express itself. The realm of social relationships also presents us with the fact that there is a relativity with respect to the possibility of expressing the Christian ideal in various forms of the social structure. Some of these patterns are better and some are worse as media of expression for the Christian life.

The fact can be illustrated if we imagine a missionary approaching a cannibalistic tribe for the purpose of Christianizing the people. The missionary could not ignore their social customs or patterns, or their cannibalistic practices in their social relationships. The absurdity of ignoring the patterns of society impresses itself upon us if we can imagine such a missionary ignoring the cannibalism of the people and simply teaching them to use a table prayer before eating. This would be a separation of the religious and the ethical. The Christian life just cannot express itself in connection with such social customs, and they must be abolished before there can be any Christian life. We cannot be indifferent to the forms and patterns of culture, if we are to take our Christian life seriously.

Another example may be taken from family relationships. The Christian ideal for marriage is monogamy. Within the framework of the monogamous family, the Christian ethic can be exercised. Many sins occur in the monogamous family relationships, but their cause is not to be found in the structure of the family relationship itself. The monogamous family pattern supplies an organization for this social unit where Christianity can be practiced. The most profound insights and experiences of the Christian can be expressed with figures from family life. The words "father," "mother," "brethren," and "sisters" come from the monogamous family relationship and are capable of symbolizing some of the deepest experiences connected with the Christian faith. The only adequate form for Christian living in the family relationship is to be found in the monogamous pattern. In other words, the structure of the family is important for the expression of the Christian life.

The doctrine of "vocation" is a tremendously dynamic concept as we meditate upon the meaning of Christian social responsibility. However, historically the life-giving stream has often vanished in the sands of the desert. It did so in Roman Catholic monasticism. It may be that monasticism arose partly as a protest against the false notion that God's forgiveness is something that can be had cheaply from God; but one of the fundamental weaknesses of monasticism is that it tries to withdraw from the ethical problem, and cuts itself off from responsible action in the world. A modern monk, describing how he found satisfaction in a Trappist monastery, used these words: "What wonderful happiness there was, then, in the world! There were still men on this miserable, noisy, cruel earth who tasted the marvelous joy of silence and solitude, who dwelt in forgotten mountain cells, in secluded monasteries, where the news and desires and appetites and conflicts of the world no longer reached them."[33] Here is an excellent illustration of a conception of "vocation" which does not lead to any sense of social responsibility.

As we look at history, we cannot be too contented over the issues of the doctrine of "vocation" in Lutheranism or Calvinism. The very emphasis on the doctrine in contemporary theology is mute testimony that the issues have not been what we should expect or would desire. Only as we come to recognize the "deadly corporateness" of sin will the dynamics of the doctrine of Christian vocation be adequately realized. Without a sense of social responsibility as we have described it, the doctrine will never be vital; but set in the framework of social responsibility, it becomes a dynamic Christian social responsibility.

There is a tendency to look upon Christian social responsibility and social action as an addendum to Christian experience. Such an attitude stems from a misunderstanding of the nature of the ethical. As man is confronted by God, he not only is made aware of his dependence but also senses his responsibility; and thus the ethical is given in the religious experience itself. The call of Moses involved a concrete content.[34] Moses was given a sense of social responsibility

---

[33] Thomas Merton, *The Seven Story Mountain* (New York: Harcourt, Brace and Company, 1948, p. 316.
[34] Exod. 3.

in that call. This concern was not a consequence of his religious experience, it was an integral part of it. The religious experience did not come first and the concern for his people and their slavery as an appendage. When Moses sensed the call of God, he was made aware that the concrete content of that call was to deliver his people from bondage. God spoke to Moses and impressed upon him a sense of social responsibility. A social interest is an integral part of religious experience, if such experience is true to the genius of the Hebrew-Christian tradition.

2

THE NEED FOR
A CHRISTIAN SOCIAL EMPHASIS

The very subject for these lectures indicates that there are those who feel that the subject needs to be emphasized. There has always been need for a social emphasis from the point of view of the Hebrew-Christian tradition. Human sin and nature being what they are, it is imperative to stress continually this aspect of our faith.

The Prophetic Recognition of Social Responsibility

The great prophets of the Old Testament, in their day, found it necessary to stress the social significance of their faith. Professor John Wick Bowman has isolated various types of religion found in the Old Testament.[1] He speaks of the religion of the altar, the religion of the book, the religion of the throne, and the religion of maturity. The latter is the great prophetic movement. The prophets were the "pioneers to Christianity," as Walter G. Williams puts it.[2]

The prophets of the Old Testament were particularly emphatic that the ethical cannot and must not be separated from vital religion. When we add to this the attitude of the prophets to superstition as a substitute for religion,[3] we dis-

[1] John Wick Bowman, *The Religion of Maturity* (Nashville: Abingdon-Cokesbury Press, 1946).
[2] Walter G. Williams, *The Prophets—Pioneers to Christianity* (Nashville: Abingdon Press, 1946).
[3] Isa. 8:19-20.

cover that the prophets exemplify the two chief roads on which, historically, religion has advanced to higher levels— the elimination of the magical and the recognition of the ethical.

The first of the great literary prophets, Amos, manifests his genius by his emphasis upon the ethical in religion. In the book of Amos we have not only monotheism, but an ethical monotheism. In a classical passage he says, as the spokesman of God, "I hate, I despise your feasts, and I will take no delight in your solemn assemblies. Yea, though ye offer me your burnt-offerings and meal-offerings, I will not accept them; neither will I regard the peace-offerings of your fat beasts. Take thou away from me the noise of thy songs; for I will not hear the melody of thy viols. But let justice roll down as waters, and righteousness as a mighty stream."[4] Here was a sense of social responsibility. A lack of justice meant death just as sure as a lack of water in the desert.

The ancient peasants called the eschatological end of all things the day of Jehovah. God would vanquish their enemies and place them in a position of supremacy. But the prophet Amos ethicized the popular eschatology, and he says, "Woe unto you that desire the day of Jehovah! Wherefor would ye have the day of Jehovah? It is darkness, and not light. As if a man did flee from a lion, and a bear met him; or went into the house and leaned his hand on the wall, and a serpent bit him. Shall not the day of Jehovah be darkness, and not light? even very dark, and no brightness in it?"[5]

What God demands of his people is social morality and justice. This is the fundamental law of the universe which God created and which is ruled by him. This was the teaching of Amos as a new way of life. We shall, perhaps, never know what the total attitude of Amos was to the cult of his day, but it is clear that he is condemning the cult as he knew

[4] Amos 5:21-24.   [5] Amos 5:18-20.

it. Dorothy Clarke Wilson has Amos looking inside the Most Holy Place in the Temple at Bethel, and when asked by the high priest if he believes that "Yahweh really lived in the little dark room" he answers, "You ought to know, you're allowed to go inside, aren't you?"[6]

The same spirit permeates the book of the prophet Isaiah. The first chapter is, perhaps, a summary of the message of the "king of the prophets," and in this chapter it is said that the herds of beasts trampling the temple courts, the burning of fat, the reek of blood, and the clouds of incense, were an abomination and a weariness to God. Festivals and solemn meetings, prayers and prostrations, were iniquity from which God turned his face. What God wanted was a right life and the righting of wrongs: ". . . your hands are full of blood. Wash you, make you clean; put away the evil of your doings from before mine eyes; cease to do evil; learn to do well; seek justice, relieve the oppressed, judge the fatherless, plead for the widow."[7]

Speaking for the Lord, Hosea said, ". . . I desire goodness, and not sacrifice . . . "[8] and Jesus was fond of quoting his words. Jesus loved Hosea and the words of the prophet are often found on his lips.

The attitude of Micah is identical. He says, "Wherewith shall I come before Jehovah, and bow myself before the high God? shall I come before him with burnt-offerings, with calves a year old? will Jehovah be pleased with thousands of rams, or with ten thousands of rivers of oil? Shall I give my first-born for my transgression, the fruit of my body for the sin of my soul? He hath showed thee, O man, what is good; and what doth Jehovah require of thee, but to do justly . . . love kindness . . . walk humbly with thy God?"[9]

6 Dorothy Clarke Wilson, *The Herdsman* (Philadelphia: Westminster Press, 1946), pp. 121 ff.

7 Isa. 1:16-17.   8 Hos. 6:6.   9 Mic. 6:6-8.

When we turn to the New Testament, we find that the first Christian martyr was charged with speaking ". . . words against this holy place, and the law . . ."; it was charged that Stephen had said ". . . that this Jesus of Nazareth shall destroy this place, and shall change the customs which Moses delivered unto us."[10] Stephen undoubtedly had been echoing the attitude of the prophets to the temple and the whole sacrificial cult.

For the apostle Paul, the whole sacrificial system was eliminated in the light of his experience with Jesus. In Romans he sublimates the whole idea when he says, "I beseech you therefore, brethren, by the mercies of God, to present your bodies a living sacrifice, holy, acceptable to God, which is your spiritual service."[11]

Without doubt we have, in the great, eighth-century prophets, an anticipation of that which came to full fruition in Jesus, Stephen, Paul, and the other New Testament writers. In these prophets we have the beginnings of an approach to the "religion of maturity" revealed in the New Testament. It is to be noted that this type of religion stresses the socially ethical aspects of life.

Priestly Religion

In order to make the emphasis which the prophetic tradition represented, it was often necessary to repudiate another type of religion, which is to be found in the Old Testament: the priestly. The prophets had to protest the cult when it became a substitute for ethical living. Admittedly, there was not a complete lack of ethical emphasis in priestly religion. Jesus quoted from the Book of Leviticus when he said ". . . thou shalt love thy neighbor as thyself . . ."[12] but the question is where the emphasis was placed.

[10] Acts 6:13-14.   [11] Rom. 12:1.   [12] Lev. 19:18.

It was the priest Amaziah who contrived to have the first of the literary prophets driven into exile,[13] and it was the high priest Caiaphas who led the opposition which finally nailed Jesus to the cross on Calvary.

The Reformation of the sixteenth century can be characterized as a break with this type of religion. The weaknesses of human nature have always tended in the direction of the development of this phenomenon, toward a priestly, cultic, and nonethical emphasis. It is always a reversion in the direction of the primitive as opposed to the "religion of maturity." Even in our own church of the Reformation, we sometimes hear the expression "parish priest" used in reference to the pastor of a congregation. Reference is sometimes made to the "priestly function" of the pastor. A pastor has the same priestly function as any other Christian, but none other. It has even been stated that when a pastor functions at the altar he is a "priest" and when he functions in the pulpit he is a "prophet." The New Testament itself repudiates this type of religion, and in our evangelical Lutheran tradition there is no room for it.

One of the most significant things about a priesthood is the idea that priesthood is a caste. This caste possesses certain extraordinary powers which make it possible to perform certain mediatorial acts other people cannot perform. The Levitical priesthood of the Old Testament is a well-known example. The priest was born into his status, and this status was determined by tribal or family considerations. After the days of Ezekiel, the sons of Zadok, by virtue of their descent, were accorded a special status in relation to other Levites. Sometimes such a status may be provided by ordination, consecration, or investiture. The emphasis here is not upon moral or spiritual considerations, or a personal prophetic call from God, but rather upon the sanctions of tradition. No

13 Amos 7:10-17.

divine call was required or claimed by the priest. His status was legitimate by virtue of his birth or investiture.

Walter Rauschenbusch has said, "The priest is the religious professional. He performs religious functions which others are not allowed to perform. It is therefore to his interest to deny the right of free access to God, and to interpose himself and his ceremonial between the common man and God. . . . It is essential to the priestly interest to establish a monopoly of rights and functions for his group. He is all for authority, and in some form or other he is always a spokesman of that authority and shares its influence. Doctrine and history as he teaches it, establish a *jure divino* institution of his order, which is transmitted either by physical descent, . . . or by spiritual descent through some form of exclusive ordination, as in the Catholic priesthood. . . . He is the middleman of religion, and like other middlemen he is sincerely convinced that he is necessary for the good of humanity and that religion would perish without him. But underneath all is the selfish interest of his class, which exploits religion."[14]

Luther completely rejected the idea of a priestly caste, and in this fact alone there should be found a dynamic for a social ethical emphasis for the Lutheran. In the *Babylonian Captivity,* he said to all who would seek holy orders through ordination: "What then is there left to you that every layman does not have? Tonsure and vestments? A sorry priest, forsooth, who consists of tonsure and vestment! . . . Let every one, therefore, who knows himself to be a Christian be assured of this, and apply it to himself, that we are all priests, and there is no difference between us; that is to say, we have the same power in respect to the Word and all the sacraments. However, no one may make use of this power

[14] Walter Rauschenbusch, *A Theology for the Social Gospel* (New York: The Macmillan Company, 1917), pp. 274-75.

except by the consent of the community or by the call of a superior. For what is the common property of all, no individual may arrogate to himself, unless he be called. And therefore this sacrament of ordination, if it have any meaning at all, is nothing else than a certain rite whereby one is called to the ministry of the Church. Furthermore, the priesthood is properly nothing but the ministry of the Word. . . ."[15]

Again Luther says, "To ordain is not to consecrate. Therefore, if we know a pious man we single him out and through the power of the Word which we possess we give him authority to preach the Word and to administer the Sacraments. This is to ordain."[16]

For Luther, the ministry of the Word was a function entrusted to certain men. All implications of caste or magic were eliminated. He did not minimize the importance of this office, even though he completely rejected the idea it was a priesthood. Again he says, "To be sure, there have been many . . . who have praised this estate highly, though more because of the saying of mass than because of preaching. This praise and glorification grew to the point where the office and estate of the priesthood (that is, of the sacrificing of the mass) was placed above Mary and the angels, because the angels and Mary could not say mass and a priest could. A new priest and his first mass were glorious, and blessed was the woman who had borne a priest; though the office of preaching is the highest and chief of all, and it was not regarded so highly. In a word, a priest was a man who could say mass, even though he did not know a word to preach and was an unlearned ass."[17] Luther thought highly of the office of the ministry, but for him it was not a priesthood—it was not a caste, limited to a particular religion or social order.

[15] *Works of Martin Luther* (6 vols.; Philadelphia: Muhlenberg Press, 1915-43), II, 282-83. Hereafter referred to as *PE*.
[16] *Ibid.*, VI, 234. [17] *Ibid.*, IV, 143.

Luther arrived at his doctrine of the ministry through his study of the New Testament. There the ministers of the Word are called prophets, apostles, evangelists, pastors, presbyters, and bishops. Never once in the New Testament is a minister of the Word called a priest. The designation "priest" is an importation, either from the Old Testament or from pagan sources. Priests are mentioned in the New Testament. Perhaps the best known are Annas and Caiaphas. Paul, Peter, James, John, and the other apostles were not the successors of Annas and Caiaphas. These ministers of the Word belonged to another significant tradition—the prophetic.

In some countries in which the Lutheran church has been established, the language itself is a source of confusion with respect to the significance of the office of the ministry. For example, in Sweden a pastor is sometimes called *prest*. Luther's knowledge of history is rather remarkable at this point. In his treatise to Emser he said, "The word 'priest' has come from the Greek, in which *presbyteros* means what *senior* means in Latin, and elder in our own tongue."[18] Archbishop Yngve Brilioth has shown clearly that presbyters became pastors of local congregations very early in the history of the church. The word *prest* in the Swedish language does not mean "priest"; it is a contraction of the word presbyter.[19] The history of the development of ecclesiastical offices in the church proves that the early church recognized no priestly caste; all such manifestations are foreign importations, and did not originally belong to the genius of the Christian faith.

In connection with one of the crises in the history of the Lutheran church in America, in 1856, the Pittsburgh Synod

[18] *Ibid.*, III, 322.
[19] Yngve Brilioth, *Svensk Kyrkokunskap* (Stockholm: Svenska Kyrkans Diakonistyrelses Bokförlag), p. 114.

adopted a paper prepared by Dr. C. P. Krauth, Jr. This reso-
lution states that "there is no priesthood on earth except
that of all believers."[20] This is the only genuine Lutheran
position and doctrine. There is a universal priesthood of
believers, and we have a great and eternal high priest in the
heavens, but there is no priestly caste on earth.

Another characteristic of priestly religion is that the priest
depends primarily upon materialistic means in order to exercise his function. Priests were primarily ministers of sacrifice. They specialized in sacrificial ritual. Their instruction
was intended primarily to teach the people about the acceptable and proper worship of God through ritual and cere-
mony. They were the cultic specialists. The use of proper
vestments (which were often of regal magnificence), the
observance of seasons, and the proper techniques of the cult
ritual, were the primary matters which engaged the attention
of the priest.

Professor Julius August Bewer characterized the difference
between the prophet and the priest when he said that both
"wanted to make the people acceptable to God. But . . . the
priests believed that it could be accomplished by ritual holi-
ness. In and through the cult they sought to educate the
people in obedience to Yahweh. . . . A purely moral and
spiritual religion was too high and exacting for the mass
of the people."[21] Professor Bowman has said that "the difference between the prophet and the priest . . . was that which
always is found to pertain between the man of vision and his
fellow of practical sense or worldly prudence, between the
statesman and the politician, the architect and the drafts-
man, the landscape artist and the gardener, the sculptor and
the stone mason. The priest . . . wrote the prophets sympho-

[20] H. K. Carroll and Others, *The American Church History Series* (13 vols.,
New York: The Christian Literature Company, 1893-97), IV, 427.
[21] Julius August Bewer, *The Literature of the Old Testament* (New York:
Columbia University Press 1922), pp. 266-67.

nies in a lower key where they could be appreciated by the
so-called 'man in the street' and stepped down the required
obedience to the divine will, which for the prophet involved
personal sacrifice, to the level of the offering of the person-
ally owned animal that had a monetary value rather than a
moral one."[22]

This does not mean that there were no priests who had a
Word of God for the people; Jeremiah and Ezekiel are examples to the contrary. But it does not mean that a priest
could function in his office without any developed sense of
moral or spiritual values, and it does mean that we often
find a tension between the prophetic and priestly type of
religion as the prophets sought to stress moral and social
values. The struggle between prophet and priest is also evident in the history of the church. The sacrifice of the Mass
is characteristic of Romanism, and the chief function of the
priest is to offer this sacrifice. The Lord's Supper is recognized as a sacrament among us, also, but there is a great
difference between the presuppositions of the "sacrifice of
the Mass" and our idea of "Communion, the Lord's Table,"
"the Sacrament of the Altar," "Abendmahl" or "Nattvard."
The "sacrifice of the Mass" and the "Sacrament of the Altar"
are not the same thing. In no sense is the pastor at the Communion service a sacrificing priest. The celebration of the
Lord's Supper is not a Protestant version of the Roman Mass.
It is something quite different.

In a priestly religion, salvation by the people was to be
attained by the right performance of certain ceremonial
rites. Interest in the cult does not necessarily mean salvation. Jesus spoke to the Samaritan woman about her salvation, and in doing so he was constrained to point to some of
the unethical aspects of her life, from which he offered her
salvation. This seems to have been rather painful for the

22 Bowman, *op. cit.,* pp. 93-94.

Samaritan woman and she immediately tried to change the subject of conversation. She commenced to question Jesus about the cult and its practices. "Our fathers worshipped in this mountain; and ye say, that in Jerusalem is the place where men ought to worship"[23] was the statement by which she tried to avoid facing the real issues of life. She was interested in the cult and in worship, but this did not mean salvation. Worship, as a cultic practice, is not a kind of filling station at which people can tank up salvation. Worship is one of the highest expressions of the human spirit but we can go through the forms, and even enjoy it, without worship in spirit and truth.

Another characteristic of the priestly religion is that it tends to emphasize the institutions of religion. The priest concerned himself primarily with the "high place," or the temple. "Trust ye not in lying words, saying, The temple of Jehovah, the temple of Jehovah, the temple of Jehovah, are these"[24] is a passage in which Jeremiah echoes the typical cry of priestly religion.

Note that we are never told in the gospels that Jesus brought any sacrifices to be offered in the temple. A sacrifice was offered in connection with his presentation in the temple, but that was an act on the part of Joseph and Mary. It is also significant that usually, when Jesus visited the Temple, conflict developed for him. Jesus never emphasized the institutions of religion. Even the word "church" was used only twice by Jesus, according to the record in the gospels. The institutions of religion are important, and religion cannot dispense with them; but they are means to an end and never ends in themselves. It is noted to be that it was the synagogue and not the temple which supplied a pattern for the worship life of the early church. Temple worship ex-

23 John 4:20.
24 Jer. 7:4.

erted some influence on the worship of the synagogue, but the function of the priest and the sacrificial cult were eliminated.

The Jewish priesthood belongs to history, and the temple, with its smoking altars, has been destroyed; but the great prophets—and Jesus, who belongs in their line of succession —survive. The prophets of the Old Testament, Langland in England, and the Reformers in Germany offered the same complaints of their priests. "God's judgment of priests is perennial," says R. F. Horton.[25]

We have devoted so much space to the prophetic and priestly type of religion because the prophets so often had to struggle against the priestly type as they emphasized God's will for social righteousness. An emphasis on the institutional church, on theology, and on the cult may all be good, but it is also possible for such emphases to produce a climate where there will be little emphasis upon social responsibility. Theology may become a sponsor for a priestly type of religion where theology is simply an attempt on the part of the church to define its self-consciousness, and where it stresses the relationship to God in such a manner that the relationship to fellow men is minimized. Religion without a social ethics is something else than our Christian faith. The scriptures themselves emphasize the need to stress the ethical in the light of perversions of the Hebrew-Christian tradition. The Roman church has developed a program for social action in various countries, together with its particular type of religion, but we cannot forget the social situation in Catholic countries like South America, Portugal, and Spain. A priestly religion and a sense of social responsibility do not necessarily exist together, and where a social emphasis is found with a priestly religion the ethical consciousness does not come from this religion.

[25] Robert Forman Horton, *The New Century Bible* (Oxford), I, 29.

Revivalism

Another type of religion which needs an emphasis upon the social ethics of scripture is revivalism. This phenomenon has been a characteristic feature of American Christianity. Camp meetings and revivals were typical of a frontier religion with Charles G. Finney and Dwight L. Moody as its representative exponents. It must be admitted that revivalism has sometimes been connected with a concern for social ethics. Modern evangelists have been known to stress social action, and we are mindful that Walter Rauschenbusch could express his appreciation of the work of Dwight L. Moody.[26] Timothy L. Smith has advanced the thesis that there was a connection between social reform and revivalism which flourished about the middle of the last century.[27] However, the type of revivalism which Smith describes preceded the period when revivalism had hardened into a particular technique. Revivalism stresses individual reception of grace as against an institutional administration of grace. Revivalism emphasizes experience as the priestly religion stresses authority—the authority of the church or the hierarchy. It ought to be an axiom, but it is often overlooked, that if individual conversion is to be socially effective, such conversion will have to be to a religion with a social emphasis. Usually, revivalism has been extremely individualistic and has failed to come to grips with the problems of society in any constructive manner. An extreme example of such individualism is found in a sermon by W. H. H. Murray, when he says, "Separate yourself from all your kind, make of the world a solitude, depopulate the globe, and think of yourself as the only living soul upon which the attention of Heaven and Hell is fixed tonight. . . . Undue importance, as it appears to me, is attached to the

26 Rauschenbusch, *A Theology for the Social Gospel*, p. 97.
27 Timothy L. Smith, *Revivalism and Social Reform* (Nashville: Abingdon Press, 1957).

connection of Christians one with another, and to the good or bad effect such connection has upon individual growth."[28] The attitude is often expressed that if people will just experience conversion to the revivalists' particular brand of religiosity, all social problems automatically will be solved. There is often an attempt to escape from the harsh realities of life. If men can only get the experience which the evangelist seeks to produce, they will be vindicated in the New Age to come. There is rarely any sense of social responsibility, and all the convert can hope for is the end of this present evil age. We are not minimizing the significance of the Christian hope for the next life; there can be a great dynamic in this hope, but it must not be separated from a sense of responsibility for the world and its problems. A vindictive delight in the destruction of the world and our own glorification are hardly an aspect of the gospel of the Lord Jesus Christ.

The Social Gospel

One movement of an earlier generation, which had the merit of recognizing the need for a Christian social emphasis, was the so-called "social gospel" movement. The year 1957 was the fiftieth anniversary of the book *Christianity and the Social Crisis* by Walter Rauschenbusch. It established the author as the greatest interpreter of the "social gospel." Reinhold Niebuhr, in his Rauschenbusch Lectures of 1934, speaks of Rauschenbusch as "the real founder of social Christianity in this country," and "its most brilliant and generally satisfying exponent to this day."[29] Walter Rauschenbusch did more than any other man in America to bring

[28] Henry Farnham May, *Protestant Churches and Industrial America* (New York: Harper and Brothers, 1949), pp. 83-84.
[29] Reinhold Niebuhr, *An Interpretation of Christian Ethics* (New York: Harper and Brothers, 1935), preface.

to the church an emphasis on Christian social responsibility.

The disciple does not always have the background of the master, and he may overemphasize, out of context, certain aspects of the doctrine of the teacher. He may also not maintain the balance of the teacher in his perspective of all the facets of the Christian faith. This undoubtedly happened among many who got their inspiration from Rauschenbusch, and the "social gospel" movement laid itself open to the criticism that it was theologically shallow. It sometimes became all "social" with very little, if any, "gospel." Sometimes it missed the real meaning of the kingdom of God in relation to history. It sometimes tended to be humanistic and lacked an emphasis upon the supernatural. There was a tendency to exalt the imminence of God at the expense of his transcendence. The conception of human nature was sometimes romantic and unrealistic, and Pelagianism was not absent as man's work took the place of divine activity. The reaction came in various types of neo-orthodoxy, and the reaction in a man like Barth was so violent that the Christian faith was removed from any relevance and relation to the world, except as God's activity is arbitrary and fortuitous. Then came Bultmann and Tillich who said that, in the light of Barth's position, we shall have to "demythologize" and reinterpret the faith in terms of human experience. The two latter theologians at least have the merit of sensing the need for contact with life.

The "social gospel" movement never did reach down to the level of the average church members. They heard about it, but it was never taken very seriously. Judging from the literature which is coming from our presses, it may be that we are on the verge of witnessing a resurgence of a social emphasis in Christian circles; but if it does arrive, it will be with a quite different theological orientation than the older "social gospel."

The term "social gospel" is, itself, a rather unfortunate expression. There is only one gospel, and that gospel is for the individual and society as well. If the term simply emphasizes a neglected aspect of the Christian faith, it may well be retained and perhaps we do need the expression in order to call attention to an aspect of the gospel which has so often been neglected. However, the social gospel is not a different gospel from the gospel for the individual. The gospel is one and inseparable for the individual and for society. The individual and the social emphasis run side by side throughout scripture.

Quietism

The Lutheran church has often been accused of quietism. At the Stockholm conference on "Life and Work," in 1925, it appeared very clearly that two types of Protestantism were represented with respect to attitudes to social responsibility. The Lutheran type was individualistic and eschatological in its orientation, emphasizing the transcendent aspects of the kingdom of God and held a rather pessimistic attitude toward the world and the social process. This group had the merit of insisting that Christian activity not be separated from divine grace, but lacked social consciousness.

The Evangelical Academy Movement developed in Germany after the close of the Second World War and it is one of the most significant attempts in German Lutheranism to develop a Christian social ethical emphasis. Many of the leaders in the movement, and in related movements in Germany, stress the fact that they have a great deal to "live down" from past history, and they are well aware of an historical quietism. The need of a social emphasis is also manifesting itself in the church in Sweden by a few voices.[30]

[30] Anders Tauson-Hassler, *Kämpande Kyrka* (Stockholm: Svenska Kyrkans Diakonistyrelses Bokförlag, 1951).

A typical attack on Lutheran quietism is that by Harris Franklin Rall when he says, "One thing we cannot do and that is to assign to religion and the Church the spiritual life of man, with some attention to social benevolence, and leave all other interests to secular control. How fateful such a conclusion could be we see when we observe its later influence, especially as illustrated in Luther and the Lutheran Movement in Germany. Here Church and state were set side by side as coordinate divine institutions. The rulers of the state presumably were to obey God and the Christian was to obey the state in all matters that concerned government and the affairs of 'the world.' True, Luther stressed the religious significance of the daily vocation, but about the total social order within which the vocation was carried on, the Church had no word to speak. But in the meantime, while the Church concerned itself with the inner and individual life, the modern age brought far-reaching changes. Industry and the nation-state grew and became mighty. Over against them the Lutheran Church with its quietism, with its separate 'spiritual' sphere in which it preached the 'pure Word,' made no pretense of challenge to the growing paganism of the social order in the name of the God who was Lord of all life. . . . Now the last stage of totalitarian statism has made plain to us that its triumph would mean the destruction of the Christian religion. Unfortunately the elements of fascism were present in western lands even before the name was coined or its logical conclusions drawn. They appeared with those who claimed for state or business a control which recognized no authority of God, no relevancy of the way of Christ, and no right of the Church to speak in regard to the social-political order."[31]

There is a dualism in Luther's thinking about spiritual

[31] Harris Franklin Rall, *According to Paul* (New York: Charles Scribner's Sons, 1945), p. 217.

and temporal power and life which has deeply influenced Lutheranism. It may be the least satisfactory aspect of Luther's thought. However, his doctrine of the "two realms" is not a dualism which manifests a consistent parallelism but the relationships of the two realms is one of interpenetration, in Luther's thinking. The spiritual and the temporal, the religious and the secular, do not run in parallel lines which never meet. H. Richard Niebuhr says, "Luther's answer to the Christ-and-culture question was that of a dynamic, dialectical thinker. Its reproductions by many who called themselves his followers were static and undialectical. They substituted two parallel moralities for his closely related ethics. . . . It is a great error to confuse the parallelistic dualism of separated spiritual and temporal life with the interactionism of Luther's gospel of faith in Christ working by love in the world of culture."[32]

Luther's thinking in this matter may have been misunderstood because the followers of Luther did not have his presuppositions. A legalistic interpretation of Luther without Luther's axioms may have given Lutheranism a different attitude to ethics than the reformer intended. No one can read Luther's treatise, an *Open Letter to the Christian Nobility,* without recognizing that Luther did not divorce Christian ethics from their social implications. In his treatise "On Trading and Usury" Luther dealt with the economic problem in the name of his religion. His interpretation of the meaning of the Fourth Petition of the Lord's Prayer is also significant in this connection. In his Catechism of 1520 the Roman tradition was followed and daily bread was interpreted to mean "the Lord Jesus Christ, who feedeth and comforteth the soul." In the edition of his Catechism of 1529 Luther had abandoned this interpretation of daily bread

---

[32] Helmut Richard Niebuhr, *Christ and Culture* (New York: Harper and Brothers, 1951), p. 179.

and includes in it "Everything that is required to satisfy our bodily needs; such as food and raiment, house and home, fields and flocks, money and goods; pious parents, children and servants; godly and faithful rulers, good government; seasonable weather, peace and health; order and honor; true friends, good neighbors and the like." In this explanation Luther certainly connected the religious interest with the problems of society. This is the more remarkable in the light of the fact that he broke with Roman Catholic tradition and thus indicates that he had considered the matter, and thus deliberately reached the conclusion to connect the religious interest with the problems of society. Whatever blame may be attached to Luther for the quietism of Lutheranism, there are aspects of his thought which point in the other direction.

Not only in Lutheranism is there need for a social ethical emphasis. F. R. Barry has said, "So completely did (Calvinism) identify religion with the nonreligious activities of spirit that it has failed to control them effectively by spiritual and religious standards. . . . Calvinist religion identified itself so completely with worldly activities as to find in the end that the world is too strong for it."[33] Max Weber was undoubtedly right when he emphasized that there was a relationship between Calvinistic ethics and the development of capitalism. His thesis may have been too simple and there may have been other factors in the development of capitalism which were more important than Weber grants, but there can be no doubt that capitalism received a good deal of inspiration from Calvinistic ethics, with its emphasis upon thrift, fitness, and energy.[34]

The ethics of the Roman church inclines to capitulate to the mores of society when the interests of the institutional

[33] F. R. Barry, *Christianity and the New World* (New York: Harper and Brothers, 1931), p. 29.
[34] Talcott Parsons (trans.), Max Weber's *The Protestant Ethic and the Spirit of Capitalism* (New York: Charles Scribner's Sons, 1958).

church are safeguarded. A former pope could be indifferent enough to the social implications of the situation to sign a concordat with Hitler and other dictators. The ethics of Calvinism has inclined toward identification with the world. The ethics of Lutheranism has tended to withdraw from the social situation. All are in need of a renewed and increased emphasis on social ethics. In the meantime, civilization may lose its soul.

3

A THEOLOGICAL POSTULATE
FOR SOCIAL RESPONSIBILITY

Various Approaches

Numerous theological approaches for social responsibility have been attempted. A biblical approach has been rather common and can never be ignored if the Bible is to be accepted as the rule of faith and practice. The Bible does emphasize social responsibility, and if the Bible is authoritative the matter is settled for the Christian.[1] The difficulty is this approach may develop into legalism when the nature of the Bible is not fully comprehended as a progressive revelation of God and his will. Very recently, biblical passages have been quoted as a justification for racial segregation.

The doctrine of justification by faith has also been used as a theological postulate for social responsibility. "In and through the process (of justification) arises the most wholesome motive for goodness in the future," says James A. Pike.[2]

[1] Abraham Cronbach, *The Bible and Our Social Outlook* (New York: The Riverdale Press, 1941); William Bennett Bizzell, *The Social Teachings of the Jewish Prophets* (New York: Riverdale Press, 1941); Charles Arthur Hawley, *The Teachings of the Prophets* (New York: Association Press, 1924); Charles Foster Kent, *The Social Teachings of the Prophets and Jesus* (New York: Charles Scribner's Sons, 1917); Walter Lee Lingle, *The Bible and Social Problems* (Union Theological Seminary, James Sprunt lectures; Westwood, N. J.: Fleming H. Revell Company, 1929); Walter Rauschenbusch, *The Social Principles of Jesus* (New York: Association Press, 1921); C. H. Dickinson, *The Social Aims of Jesus* (West Rindge, N.H.: Richard R. Smith, Inc., 1930); B. C. Plowright, *Rebel Religion* (Los Altos, California: Round Table Press, Inc., 1937).

[2] James A. Pike, *Doing the Truth* (Garden City, N.Y.: Doubleday and Company, 1955).

Albert Schweitzer has said that "Western theology is mainly concerned with the doctrine of the forgiveness of sins, and its task is to interpret the death of Jesus in such a way that men may find in it forgiveness ever available, ever renewed, for all the lapses of which they become guilty."[3] This doctrine is a very important doctrine and it is a specific article in the Apostles' Creed itself. Without forgiveness there is no reconciliation with God for man. We must not detract from the significance of this doctrine, but we ought to use it in the framework of the whole New Testament faith. The Second Article of the Creed is important but there is a First and a Third Article, as well. If we neglect to emphasize the First Article, it will be difficult to deal with the Third Article, because it is in God's creation that the life of sanctification is to be lived. Luther stressed the doctrine of justification as the pearl of great price, but Luther had a great variety of theological axioms which he took for granted and held in common even with his adversaries. When some of Luther's followers make use of his writings as a kind of legal code (while lacking the axioms which he held) they arrive at quite a different position from Luther and what he contemplated.

Another theological approach to social responsibility has been the doctrine of "vocation." We have already pointed out that this approach has not proved dynamic in the light of history. It is also significant that the idea of an "earthly calling" is found only once in the New Testament. In I Cor. 7:20 Paul says, "Let each man abide in that calling wherein he was called." Here the word undoubtedly is used to refer to man's station in life. This fact is significant for those who seek a theological nexus between religion and the problems of society in the doctrine of "vocation." Such an emphasis is

[3] E. N. Mozley, *The Theology of Albert Schweitzer for Christian Inquirers* (New York: The Macmillan Company, 1950), p. 94.

a rather modern innovation. In the New Testament the term is used in an almost exclusively religious sense, and has reference to the call of the Christian to share in the salvation which God offers in Christ.[4]

The Kingdom of God

There is a theological concept in the scriptures which inevitably leads to a sense of social responsibility. This concept is the "kingdom of God." When the meaning of the kingdom of God is grasped, religion immediately becomes social in its outlook because the kingdom of God is, in itself, a social concept. Many years ago I determined to find out what those who manifested a sense of social responsibility had, theologically, that was absent in those who failed to emphasize the social responsibility of the Christian. The answer was not difficult to find. Almost invariably a sense of social responsibility was connected with an insight into the meaning of the kingdom of God.

Toyohiko Kagawa, the famous Japanese Christian, says, "The kind of Christianity which makes me want to save myself alone is useless."[5] He had been a leader in the labor movement and in the co-operative movement in Japan. He initiated the Kingdom of God movement in his country. The kingdom of God became, for Kagawa, a dynamic for social action.

The New Testament exegesis of Walter Rauschenbusch is subject to revision in the light of modern New Testament scholarship but he, too, made the kingdom of God central in his thinking, and that insight is a permanent and vital contribution for all time. He says, "If theology is to offer an adequate doctrinal basis for the social gospel, it must not

4 Rom. 11:29; Phil. 3:14; II Thess. 1:11; Eph. 1:18; II Tim. 1:9; II Pet. 1:10.
5 Toyohiko Kagawa, *Meditations on the Cross* (Chicago: Willett Clark and Company, 1935), p. 37.

only make room for the doctrine of the Kingdom of God, but
give it a central place."[6] The Brotherhood of the Kingdom
was organized by Rauschenbusch at Rochester when he commenced to teach there, and this fellowship exerted a far-
reaching influence.

Albert Schweitzer has sensed the meaning of the kingdom
of God for the Christian faith. His activity has been confined
largely to the remedial realm, but the motivation and inspiration of the meaning of the Kingdom of God is evident
in his life work. He says that "whenever the idea of the
Kingdom of God is no longer at the center of faith . . . (it)
has led to far-reaching impoverishment."[7] Furthermore, he
says, originally "Christianity had been the religion of faith
in the Kingdom of God."[8] In the same vein he says, "Originally, the dominant thought of the Kingdom of God meant
that believers shared with one another the blessings of a new
creation. But (then) the experience of the individual (began to take) precedence of that of the community. Each
separate believer . . . (came to be) concerned with his own
redemption. He cares nothing for the future of mankind and
of the world. There is something cold and unnatural about
the naive egoism of such piety."[9] He also says that, "Only
as it comes to be understood as something ethical and spiritual . . . can the Kingdom of God regain, in our faith, the
force that it had for Jesus and the early Church. Christianity
must have a firm hold of this, if it is to remain true to itself,
as it was at the beginning—religion dominated by the Kingdom of God."[10] Again he says, in a classical passage, "Belief
in the Kingdom of God makes the biggest demands of all
the articles of the Christian faith. It means believing the

[6] Walter Rauschenbusch, *A Theology for the Social Gospel*, p. 131.
[7] Mozley, *op. cit.*, p. 91.
[8] *Ibid.*, p. 92.
[9] *Ibid.*, p. 90.
[10] *Ibid.*, p. 110.

seemingly impossible—the conquest of the spirit of the world by the Spirit of God. We look with confidence for the miracle to be wrought through the Spirit."[11]

One of the relatively few modern evangelists with a social message is E. Stanley Jones. His concern about the problems of the laboring man, racial equality, and war and peace, are evident in all his books. In all of his writings the dominant note is the kingdom of God. One of his books bears the title *Is the Kingdom of God Realism?* Here, too, an emphasis upon the kingdom of God and a social interest are inseparably united.

In 1925, the ecumenical conference on "Life and Work" convened in Stockholm. This conference devoted its attention to what its name designated; namely, life and work. It may have been a loss to the Christian cause that "Faith and Order" and "Life and Work" were united at the Oxford conference. Archbishop Nathan Soderblom was the leader at the Stockholm conference, and Soderblom was a theologian with a greater sense of social responsibility than is usually found among Swedish theologians. He published a volume on the conference, and he designated the outstanding question of the conference as having been the meaning of the kingdom of God.[12] The delegates could not come to grips with the problems of life and work without consideration of the meaning of the kingdom of God. This again illustrates how intimately the idea of the kingdom of God is connected with the social mission of the church.

The kingdom of God expresses the very essence of Christ's life purpose. It was the key phrase of Jesus' teaching and message. He made use of the phrase from the beginning to the end of his ministry. The Sermon on the Mount centers in this theme. Those who live in the light of the presence

11 *Ibid.*, p. 116.
12 Nathan Söderblom, in *Kristenhetens Möte i Stockholm* (Stockholm: Svenska Kyrkans Diakonistyrelses Bokförlag, 1926), p. 233 ff.

of the kingdom of God are following in the footsteps of Jesus and are dominated by the spirit which was in him. The kingdom of God was a central concept for Jesus, and to deny this would be the equivalent of denying that we have any reliable information about the mind which was in Christ Jesus.

The phrase is not so common in the epistles of the New Testament as it is in the Synoptic Gospels. However, Paul's letters were usually written in response to certain specific problems, and we cannot draw the conclusion from his letters that he minimized the preaching of the kingdom of God. To the elders of the church at Ephesus, Paul said that he had gone about "preaching the kingdom," according to his devoted friend, Luke.[13] Likewise, in the last glimpse which we get of the apostle in the Book of Acts, we are told that "he abode two whole years in his own hired dwelling, and received all that went in unto him, preaching the kingdom of God . . ."[14]

What, then, is the kingdom of God? Archbishop Soderblom has defined the concept of the kingdom in the following words: "The Kingdom of God is the sovereignty of God. The Kingdom of God means the realm where God rules—in the heart of man, in the social life of peoples, in greater and smaller organizations (*samfund*), in humanity and in existence in its entirety."[15] Walter Rauschenbusch says, "The Kingdom of God is humanity organized according to the will of God."[16] The horizons of Walter Rauschenbusch were so wide that one must be careful not to quote him out of context, but if we compare Soderblom's definition with this statement by Rauschenbusch we recognize quite a dif-

[13] Acts 20:25.
[14] Acts 28:30-31.
[15] Nathan Söderblom, *Jesu Bergspredikan* (Stockholm: P. A. Norstedt & Söners Firlag, 1926), p. 2.
[16] Rauschenbusch, *A Theology for the Social Gospel*, p. 142.

ferent orientation. Soderblom does not leave the social scene untouched by the kingdom of God, but he would undoubtedly never have said what Rauschenbusch did. It is extremely important to keep clearly in mind, as Soderblom did, that God's kingdom is God's activity.

God is the absolute sovereign in his creation and is active in history, accomplishing his good purposes. God is not geographically transcendent, in any faraway manner, waiting on some celestial throne to be discovered by man. He is living and active and makes himself known through his activity and sovereignty. The kingdom of God is the rule of God in the hearts and lives of men. The kingdom of God is always coming and pressing in upon the present. It is the very energy of God pressing in upon human affairs. It is the "eternal" in the midst of time, and it is both present and future. The powers of the kingdom of God were supremely present in the person of Jesus.

The Kingdom of God in the Book of Daniel

One of the most significant descriptions of the meaning of the kingdom of God is to be found in the Book of Daniel. It is fundamental for an understanding of the New Testament conception of the kingdom. Chapter VII of that book is one of the more important chapters of scripture. The Babylonian, the Median, the Persian, and the Greek kingdoms are represented by four beasts who "came up from the sea." Anyone familiar with the symbolism of Babylonian mythology, and that of Psalms 8, 74, 89, 93, 95, 96, 97, and 98, will recognize the source of the imagery which was used by the author of the Book of Daniel. There can be little doubt that the Babylonian myth of creation supplied much of the symbolism used in these Psalms as well as in the Book of Daniel. The Babylonian myth related how the world was

created when Marduk, the chief Babylonian deity, slew
Tiamat, the great sea monster, who represented the powers
of Chaos. Tiamat, Rahab, Leviathan, and the monsters coming up out of the sea were opposed to the rule of God and
represented the enemies of God. These monsters were attempting to undo the work of God's creation and reduce the
world to chaos. They were set against God and his creative
purposes.

However, these monsters are not outside the control of
God. Although the heathen nations still roar, they will be
subdued; for the "ancient of days did sit" upon his throne,
and the monsters will have their dominion taken away. Set
against the destructive beasts are the power and purpose of
God, who will ultimately subdue all things to himself. Evil
is arraigned before the heavenly court of God and judgment
is passed upon the arrogant kingdoms of the world.

The figure of the Son of Man also enters the picture. The
beasts represent kingdoms opposed to the rule of God. The
Son of Man represents the people in whom the sovereignty
of God is to be manifested, and through whom the rule of
God on earth is to be revealed. Dominion is to be taken
away from the beasts and given to the Son of Man. In the
Book of Daniel, the Son of Man represents the faithful
people of Israel, but any student of the gospels will recall
that one of the favorite phrases with which Jesus identified
himself was—the Son of Man. He was the representative of
God who created the world, and he has a function to fulfill
in the judgment and restoration of the world. He appears
upon the stage of history, and he will defeat the powers of
evil. Through the Son of Man, the kingdom of God comes;
and God's sovereignty over his creation will be established.
The coming of the Son of Man and the coming of the kingdom are identified.

The majestic symbolism of the Book of Daniel presents

God as Creator, Redeemer, Judge, and King. The God of Creation is none other than the God of Redemption and the two must be identified theologically. Creation and Redemption are not distinct and unrelated activities of God but are both manifestations of the same sovereignty of God. The New Testament is equally insistent upon maintaining this connection.[17] Theology ignores it at its peril. God has not abandoned his creation to those who are opposed to his will. He is active in his world and history, and his kingdom is a dynamic reality through which he is working out his purposes. The radiant and venerable Judge sits upon his throne and ultimate authority belongs to him. This is the meaning of the phrase, "The kingdom of God." God *is* Creator, Redeemer, Judge, and King. In this framework every doctrine of the Christian faith should be set. If we isolate any one of these aspects of the divine activity from the others, it will carry with it dire consequences for theology and the Christian life. The ethical teaching of Jesus is inextricably bound up with this view of God's kingdom. In the final analysis, God's will is sovereign over all men and the whole of creation; and the implications of this point of view, for social responsibility, are too apparent to need explication. We cannot understand the meaning of the kingdom of God and fail to see its implications for the social order. God is making something out of his creation.

The Kingdom as a Gift

It is God who exercises his sovereignty and, therefore, his kingdom is his gift. It is something "given." The sovereignty of God does not depend upon man's will or activity. At no place in the New Testament are we told to "build the kingdom." It is already established "from the foundations of the

17 John 1:3; Col. 1:16.

world." We can "see . . . enter . . . proclaim" and "suffer"
for it. But we cannot build it. The kingdom is something
to be accepted, submitted to, and obeyed. The rulers of this
world have their day, but the ultimate authority is God's.
God is King; and Jesus, as the absolute revelation of God,
exercises a kingly office.

Human Responsibility

If this be the nature of the kingdom, then what of human
responsibility? And we *are* concerned about responsibility in
this series of lectures.

Neither activism nor quietism is an answer to our question. The Christian will not become passive to responsibilities in the social order and simply wait for a celestial relief
expedition. There are types of modern theology which leave
the impression that the theologian is interested in the doctrine of creation and in the doctrine of the parousia, but
expects nothing to happen between those poles. This attitude
involves the thought that despair and defeatism are the only
realistic attitudes with respect to the whole realm of history.
Extra-canonical apocalytic supplies historical background for
this attitude.

The Christian does have a responsibility for the character
of society because he has been laid hold of by the powers
of the kingdom, and those powers work in and through him.
Paul realized it was God who was bringing in his kingdom,
but that fact did not release Paul from a tremendous missionary task. Paul could say, "It is God who worketh in you both
to will and to work," but he could also speak of his "labor"
for the Lord.[18] The prophets of the Old Testament often
spoke of the Exodus from Egypt as the work of God,[19] but

18 Phil. 2:13, 16.
19 Amos 9:7.

Moses was given a task to perform in connection with that deliverance. God performed his deliverance through the instrumentality of a man. A secular historian might write an account of the Exodus from the point of view of the leadership afforded by Moses, but the sacred historian sees, back of the human instrumentality, the movements of God in history. C. T. Craig has well said, "The message of the Kingdom (of God) does not deal with our social task but with God's saving act. This fact should never be made an excuse for quietism. If Jesus saw in his healing ministry 'signs' of the coming of the kingdom, we may interpret signal victories of social and economic justice in similar fashion. Though the perfected rule of God never comes completely into time, it is still always possible to attain a more Christian social order. The resistance of man's radical sinfulness should never plunge us into defeatism and despair. Though our faith is not *in* man we must retain hope *for* man. It is possible to taste here and now something of the powers of the age to come" (Heb. 6:5).[20] The kingdom is a gift, but the powers of the kingdom operate through human agents. The kingdom is the supreme gift of God, but by virtue of this, it also becomes for each of us, our supreme task. God establishes his kingdom, but in so doing he takes us into his service. Man's activity in the interest of the kingdom of God is God's activity in man. To wait for the coming of the kingdom in the spirit of quietism is not true to the genius and the dynamic power of the Christian faith. A gift is bestowed upon us, but that gift involves a call to a task in which God uses men as his instruments. This task is more than an effort to help men understand themselves and God's will for them as individuals. It involves the whole realm of history and society, and the transformation of human institutions for human betterment.

[20] Clarence Tucker Craig, "The Teaching of Jesus," in *The Interpreter's Bible* (12 vols.; Nashville: Abingdon-Cokesbury Press, 1952), VII, 153.

Freedom

The fact of human responsibility also poses the question about freedom. The highest type of freedom is Christian freedom. Christian freedom is not license. It is not liberty to sin and then trust in the goodness of God for forgiveness. The grace of God is no cloak for maliciousness. Christian liberty consists in the agreement of the human and the divine will. When man is laid hold of by the powers of the kingdom, there will be constraint but no restraint. Man is made free by being bound in the will of God. Paul was the bond servant of Jesus Christ, but at the same time he was free. Freedom exercised so as to violate the laws of health does not lead to real freedom. It leads, rather, to bondage under disease. In like manner, freedom does not consist in the ability to sin, but in finding oneself in harmony with God and his will. Little man cannot dethrone God or deprive him of his sovereignty. God's kingdom is not dependent upon man's consciousness of that kingdom. God rules, either in judgment or in mercy, and no man can escape the "hound of Heaven"; and the only real freedom there is must be found in harmony with his will. Every other relationship is bondage under sin.

The position taken above involves a paradox. Calvin tried to deal with the matter in a logical manner and arrived at his doctrine of double predestination. The most significant thing about the doctrine of double predestination is that it says there is no logical solution for the question of the relationship of divine sovereignty to human responsibility. From the point of view of the Christian faith, we are conscious of both divine sovereignty and human responsibility—and we must assert the reality of both. Here we leave the matter, and if life and experience are not logical it will have to be too bad for logic. Divine activity and sovereignty do not override human responsibility and freedom. It uses them to serve the divine will.

A Philosophy of History

Faith in the kingdom of God gives the Christian a vital philosophy of history. A philosophy of history involves an attitude to, and a determination of, the forces which fashion man's history, and a consideration of the means involved in securing the predetermined goals. The prophets and the apocalyptists both had their philosophy of history, but with a difference. H. H. Rowley says, "Whereas the prophets believed in the divine initiative and control in all history, the apocalyptists seem to reserve it for the great final act of history. I do not think this is quite fair to them (the apocalyptists), however. Their supreme interest is in the great final act of history, and they wish to set that act, in all its uniqueness, in sharp relief against all the history that has preceded it. I do not think they would have denied the hand of God in all history, for they certainly did not repudiate the teaching of the prophets. But they looked at all the course of human history merely from the human side, as the record of human lust for power and oppression and ruthlessness, until they came to the final denouement of history, which was regarded solely and uniquely as the act of God. (Here God) would Himself act in a way as solely his own as His act in creation had been. . . . Hence, for the apocalyptists to have emphasized the divine hand in all history would have obscured the uniqueness of this expected act of God."[21]

Rowley does offer a legitimate apologetic for some of the apocalyptic writers, but it is also true that, generally speak-

---

[21] H. H. Rowley, *The Relevance of Apocalyptic* (New York: Harper and Brothers, 1955), pp. 154-55.

ing, "the apocalyptic scheme was not a product of pure Hebrew thought, but an exotic growth. In fact, its dualism and transcendentalism were a radical departure from Hebrew religion."[22] Apocalypticism produced a prolific literature, but out of this great mass of literature only two books found their way into the canon of scripture—the Book of Daniel in the Old Testament, and the Book of Revelation in the New Testament. We have shown that there is an emphasis in both of these books on the activity of God in history, and this may be one of the chief reasons why these books found their place in the canon. The apocalyptic books which lacked this emphasis were excluded. The Hebrew-Christian tradition sees God not only above and at the end of history, but in the processes of history itself. Isaiah could speak of the Assyrian as the rod of God's anger and the staff in whose hand was God's indignation.[23] Any interpretation of history which excludes God from the processes of history does not have its origin in biblical faith. The realm of history is also the realm of social responsibility. Apocalypticism, with its dualism and transcendentalism, have been particularly influential in much modern theological thinking, and this has not been conducive to any emphatic social emphasis. Neo-orthodoxy is often at fault in failing to recognize this fact, and it has sometimes tended to make the devil the lord of history. We shall have to take the realm of history seriously as a stage for divine activity if we are adequately to sense our social responsibility. In the Book of Daniel, God not only manifests his sovereignty at the end of the age,[24] but the kings Nebuchadnezzar, Belshazzar, Darius, and Cyrus are also subject to the control of God. The power and the kingdom of God manifest themselves not only at the end

[22] Walter Rauschenbusch, *Christianizing the Social Order* (New York: The Macmillan Company, 1912), p. 56.
[23] Isa. 10:5.
[24] Dan. 2:34, 35, 44.

of the age or in the crises of history, they are always a present reality. To believe that God is in ultimate control of the forces of history is one of the most challenging articles of the Christian faith. We stand in need of an emphasis upon the relation of the kingdom of God to the historical process, and we can never be satisfied with a theology which attempts to explain away this connection. God is the Lord of history —not only at the end, but in the process itself. Our God is the God of religious experience; he is the God of eternity, but he is also the God of time and history.[25] This does not mean that every specific event of history is a product of God's will, because the fact of human sin can deflect the course of history from a full realization of God's good will. It does mean, however, what the author of the Book of Job has in mind when he says for the Lord:

> "Hitherto shalt thou come, but no further;
> And here shall thy proud waves be stayed."[26]

Hegel had his philosophy of history. He absolutized the state and made the state a kind of incarnation of the divine idea as it exists on earth. Karl Marx had his philosophy of history. For Marx, the economic productive forces make up the power which determines the course of history. The Greeks had their cycle theory of history, and Oswald Spengler has, in modern times, resurrected this theory. Fascism, free enterprise, and the "American way," all have their conscious or unconscious philosophies as to what determines the course of historical development. Against these philosophies of history stands the Christian faith, and it insists that the ultimate determining factor for human history is the kingdom of God. To believe this, means to believe in a moral determinism of history; for God is not only power,

25 Isa. 40:12-31.
26 Job 38:11.

he is also an ethical Being. One of the greatest advances in the history of religion occurred when men came to see God in terms of the ethical. History is not blind fate, but behind history is God and his kingdom. This is a faith on the basis of which we can face the human predicament of our time.

The Christian Hope

In some philosophies of history the idea of progress has played a significant role. Under the influence of the biological evolution theory, society has been thought of in terms of a gradual advance toward an ideal state. The idea played a very important part in liberal theology, and one of the sharpest criticisms by neo-orthodoxy has been aimed at the idea of progress. Much of this criticism has been justified, but there were some religious values in the concept which need to be re-emphasized lest the baby be thrown out with the wash water. The concept of progress did have the merit that it took the realm of history seriously.

Often there was a naive optimism associated with the idea of progress. Two world wars and a terrible depression in the economic area have tended to shake such optimism. The alternative, however, is not a pessimism which would forget a God who is living and active in the realm of human history. In his *Decline of the West,* Oswald Spengler says, "Time does not suffer itself to be halted; there is no question of prudent retreat or wise renunciation. Only dreamers believe there is a way out. Optimism is cowardice. We are born into this time and must bravely follow the path to the predestined end. There is no other way. Our duty is to hold on to the lost position—without hope, without rescue—like that Roman soldier whose bones, found in Pompey, showed that during the eruption of Vesuvius he died at his post because his superiors forgot to relieve him. That is greatness. That is what it means to be a thoroughbred. The honorable end is the one thing that cannot be taken from man."[27] Here is a philosophy of history without the idea of progress and without hope. Here is a philosophy without consciousness of God and in the spirit of the deepest pessimism. It foregoes its right to "wonder why" for do and die.

Instead of talking about progress, as Christians we can talk about hope. ". . . now abideth faith, hope, love, . . ."[28] says the apostle Paul. Faith and hope belong together. Hope is simply our faith projected into the future. We have hope because of our faith in God and what we know about him. Our hope is not a "fool's paradise" but is anchored in our knowledge of God and his kingdom. Hope is the expectation of the good. It is directed to something not yet realized. The Christian hope extends to the realm beyond history, but it also involves history. We are not beating the air as Christians when we find ourselves committed to a realization of the will of God on earth. We hope—and we believe—that more of the gracious and good will of God can be realized on earth and in the realm of history than is now prevalent. This hope is not an air castle, but a firm conviction. It is not based upon the development of means of mass destruction, but upon obedience to God and his will. It is a strange phenomenon that, at a time when some of the secular philosophies of history should be holding forth a hope for society, popular theological trends should be gripped by the spirit of despair for the social order. There is hope *for* history and *in* history, because God is a living and active God even in the realm of history. The apocalyptic hope of communism must be challenged by our Christian hope, or the appeal of our preaching and teaching is not going to be significantly vital. God's reign in his creation and history must not be abandoned

[27] Oswald Spengler, *Decline of the West* (2 vols.; New York: Alfred A. Knopf, Inc., 1945).
[28] I Cor. 13:13.

in theology. The meaning of God's kingdom for history requires a renewed emphasis in our day.

This position does not involve perfectionism. The Christian hope involves the whole doctrine of Christian eschatology, and the historical process itself does not contain the eschatological goal. However, the eschatological goal is always relevant for the historical situation. It always stands over against us, in judgment and as a guiding star. The North star was important for the sailor even though he never reached it. So the ideals of the kingdom of God are always relevant for the social order. They mark the direction in which our hope is to seek realization. Socially, our Christian hope is realized in the measure in which Christian ideals become increasingly possible.[29] James Orr said, long ago, that "Christianity, and more particularly the Christian idea of the Kingdom of God, furnish the only solid ground for (hope) for mankind."[30] The kingdom of God means hope for society.

The question is often asked: To what extent will the ideals of the kingdom of God be realized in the historical process? The answer is: we do not know. Furthermore, we have not been called to succeed; we have been called to be faithful. How much of his good will God will realize in history is within his good counsel. Our responsibility is to be faithful to our task. We cherish the hope that God—in us and through us—will realize more of his will on earth than is now the case.

Degrees of Sin and Guilt

If we are not to fall into the perils of perfectionism, this attitude involves degrees of guilt. One of the ways in which some forms of neo-orthodoxy have undermined a sense of

[29] Alfred N. Whitehead, *The Adventures of Ideas* (New York: The Macmillan Company).

[30] James Orr, *The Christian View of God and the World* (Grand Rapids, Mich.: Wm. B. Eerdmans Publishing Company, repr. 1947), p. 454.

social responsibility has been through a denial of the inequality of sins and guilt. Classical Christian theology has always recognized this distinction. Sins were classified as *graviora et leviora*. There is good New Testament authority for this position. Jesus said to Pilate, ". . . he that delivered me unto thee hath greater sin."[31] The word "greater" is a comparative. Matthew 11:24, Luke 12:48-49, and Matthew 12:29-34 are other classical examples of degrees of guilt.

One of the favorite passages for those who would deny the fact of degrees of sin and guilt is James 2:10, where the author says, "Whosoever shall keep the whole law, and yet stumble in one point, he is become guilty of all." This passage of scripture does not deny the fact of the degrees of sin and guilt, but refers rather to the essence of sin. One deliberate choice of sin indicates that the personality is evil and disposed to sin. If a man willfully transgresses one commandment, it shows that in principle he disregards all. Actual transgression of one commandment involves potential transgression of all the commandments.

George F. Thomas has made some significant remarks on this subject, among them: "There has been a strong tendency in orthodox Protestantism to reject the doctrine of the inequality of sin on the ground that it encourages man's pride and self-sufficiency. Most recently, Reinhold Niebuhr has asserted 'the equality of sin' while admitting the 'inequality of guilt.' According to his view, guilt 'represents the objective and historical consequences of sin,' and it is a plain fact that while men are equal in their sin, the consequences of their sin are very unequal. This position cannot be maintained. In the first place, there seems to be no biblical basis for it. For example, the statement of St. Paul, 'For there is no distinction; since all have sinned, and fall short of the glory of God,' is not to the point. It asserts that there is no

31 John 19:11.

difference between men with respect to the presence of sin in their lives, but not that there is no difference between them with respect to the degree of sin; that is, it asserts the universality rather than the equality of sin. In the second place, the guilt of a person is more closely related to his sin than Niebuhr's view recognizes. If the guilt of two men is unequal, it can be only because their sins are unequal. For if sin is the ground of guilt, there must be degrees of sin to account for degrees of guilt. To say that the greater guilt assigned to a person is due simply to the fact that his acts have worse consequences for others, is to estimate guilt in too external and utilitarian fashion; and to transform guilt from a moral, into a legal, category. The conclusion follows that, if there is inequality of guilt, there must also be inequality of sin."[32]

This doctrine must never be used in the interest of self-righteousness, but it is a tremendously important aspect of Christian anthropology. Growth in sanctification and its possibility are recognized by this doctrine. If the Christian cannot be perfect in this life, and if there are no degrees of sin and guilt, the conclusion is inevitable that there can be no growth "unto the measure of the stature of the fulness of Christ: . . ."[33] In like manner, if we cannot expect a full realization of the ideals of the kingdom of God in history, we shall be reduced to a simple holding operation, unless there be inequality in sins and guilt. Our Christian hope involves that we can attain to more than we have. If we destroy this aspect of hope, the whole realm of social responsibility becomes meaningless. The attacks of some modern theologians upon the doctrine of degrees of sin and guilt are another example of the manner in which some types of contemporary theology whittle away at the ethical

---

[32] George F. Thomas, *Christian Ethics and Moral Philosophy* (New York: Charles Scribner's Sons, 1955), p. 184.
[33] Eph. 4:13.

contents of the Christian faith. The fifth petition of the Lord's Prayer will undoubtedly continue to be meaningful to the end of time, but this does not mean that we eliminate the categories of less and more. The black reality of human sin does not obscure the fact that there may be more or less of it.

The realm of history is His story, and His kingdom gives us our social responsibility. For the Christian faith, the kingdom of God is a present reality; and from the point of view of that reality we view all of life, individual as well as social. ". . . the kingdom of God is at hand: repent ye, and believe in the gospel"[34]—*this* gospel.

[34] Mark 1:15.

4

A NORM FOR CHRISTIAN
SOCIAL RESPONSIBILITY

An examination of a goodly number of ethical treatises written during the last quarter of a century will give the impression that it is hopeless to attempt a systematic presentation of a Christian ethic. Neither reason, natural law, nor scripture provides us with principles so we can arrive at Christian duties and virtues which are normative.[1]

The position is sometimes maintained that the ultimate standard for the Christian life is the Christian himself. In the first place the statement is not true, because the ultimate standard is to be found in the will of God. In the second place, the statement says precisely nothing with respect to the concrete content of the Christian life.

The Need of Law and Moral Principle

We cannot allow ourselves to fall into such obscurantism that we deprive ourselves of any means of discriminating between what is good and what is evil. We must come to grips with the problem and determine the manner in which we, as Christians, are to resist and reform the corporate orders of existence. A statement of principle and policy is

[1] Emil Brunner, *The Divine Imperative* (Philadelphia: Westminster Press, 1947); Reinhold Niebuhr, *Moral Man and Immoral Society* (New York: Charles Scribner's Sons, 1952); Werner Elert, *The Christian Ethos* (Philadelphia: Muhlenberg Press, 1957).

imperative or we shall have an ethics without vitality. Whence, how, and with what content, are questions which ethics cannot ignore. Unless we give some kind of answer to the question "How is the Christian ethic to be made effective in society?" we shall not be meaningful in our sense of social responsibility. There are those who would say that the answer to our problem is that the Christian lives his life in the light of the constant presence of God. We cannot quarrel with such a statement, but we still need some way of describing what this means in concrete terms of action. Moral principles do have their function in ethical decisions and ethics cannot dispense with them and remain vital. Love is a motivating power for good but the good has to be discriminated. Moral principles and categories are an imperative for any vital ethics. Love must be related to the concrete social situation, and this cannot be done without some sense of moral principles. All law or principle—from the point of view of the New Testament—must be interpreted in the light of the ethics of love, but principles are an interpretation of the meaning of love. Law is an expression of moral principle, and Paul, the great apostle of justification by faith, could say, "Do we then make the law of none effect through faith? God forbid: nay, we establish the law."[2] The assumption of antinomians—that without moral principles love would discover what is moral in each concrete situation—is just not realism. What men have seen as the will of God, in their historical experience, we ignore at our peril. Moral principles do not give us detailed information with respect to duty in every situation, but they do suggest the right direction for our conduct. To ignore the experience of the race in this realm is as great a folly as to do so in any other realm. We are not hesitant to use the word "principle," because the word describes an attitude; and only through

[2] Rom. 3:31.

the recognition of moral principle can the contents of the Christian ethic be communicated. Moral principle also has its value in giving direction for social action. Perhaps, also, we ought to remind ourselves that the Christian man is not wholly Christian in his sanctification, and moral principle and law are bound to be significant for him in this respect also.

Description of the Ethical

How, then, shall we describe the principle which is normative for Christian social responsibility? The moral philosophers, from Plato onward, have recognized that "the good for man must reside in that which completely harmonizes and most nearly brings to full fruition all his powers, capacities, and endowments."[3] Smyth says, "that is moral which at any time tends to preserve the life of man in its largest capacity and efficiency."[4] Martensen defines the ethical ideal as "human personality conceived in its purity and perfection."[5] Undoubtedly, Albert Schweitzer had the same idea in mind when he wrote, "I see that evil is what annihilates, hampers, or hinders life. Goodness . . . is the saving or helping of life, the enabling of whatever life I can to attain its highest development."[6] Undoubtedly, too, Schweitzer includes more in the term "life" than do most ethical thinkers, but he would doubtless include the definitions given above in his definition of the term. The fourth Gospel quotes Jesus himself as saying, ". . . I came that they may have life, and may have it abundantly."[7]

[3] Frank Russell Barry, *Christianity and the New World* (New York: Harper and Brothers, 1931), p. 141.
[4] Newman Smyth, *Christian Ethics* (New York: Charles Scribner's Sons, 1903), p. 86.
[5] C. Spence (trans. and ed.), D. Martensen's *Christian Ethics* (Edinburgh: T & T Clark, 1873), p. 3.
[6] As quoted in now defunct magazine *Christendom*, I(2), 230.
[7] John 10:10.

The Law of God

The law of God is a description, in concrete terms, of the will of God. God reveals himself and his will, and man describes his experience of revelation in the form of law or principle. The law and its relation to Christian living have been subject to a great deal of debate in theological circles during the last quarter of a century. The so-called third use of the law, which has reference to the relation of the Christian to the law, has sometimes been denied, sometimes minimized, and sometimes included in the first use of the law, which has to do with civic righteousness. A certain antinomianism in modern theology is apparent, also, in this attitude and attacks the very foundations of Christian ethics. The Christian faith is something more than a "consolation for the misery of sin"—to use Harnack's phrase. The law of God, as a description of his will, is significant for the Christian. The Lutheran Confessions emphasize this when they say the law is one and the same, to wit: "the unchangeable will of God, whether it be set forth before the penitent or the impenitent, the regenerate or the unregenerate . . . we reject and condemn, as pernicious and contrary to Christian discipline and true godliness, the erroneous doctrine that the law in the manner and treasure indicated above is not to be urged upon Christians and true believers but only upon unbelievers, non-Christians, and the unrepentant."[8] It is also significant that the keeping of the law should be described in this article as one of "the fruits of the Spirit." In like manner, Luther says, "But the spirit, which is divine grace, gives strength and power to the heart, yea, creates a new man, who grows to love God's commandments and does with joy all that he ought to do. . . . By this . . . grace a man does what the law commands and satisfies it."[9]

[8] Theodore G. Tappert (trans.), "Formula of Concord, Article VI," *The Book of Concord* (Philadelphia: Muhlenberg Press, 1959), pp. 563-68.
[9] *PE*, III, 354-55.

Therefore a concrete place must be given to the law as an expression of God's will for his people.

An antinomianism which would "make void the law through faith," as someone has said, does not belong to the classical Christian tradition. Some forms of Gnosticism would have been hospitable to it. As antinomianism can manifest itself in connection with an emphasis upon faith, so it can also manifest itself in connection with an emphasis upon agape, or love. The antinomian divorces religion from morality and morality from religion. Christianity has always had to be on guard against this tendency. There is an echo of the spirit of antinomianism in the words of the New Testament, "All things are lawful for me; . . ." and in the words "Meats for the belly, and the belly for meats: . . ." in I Cor. 6:12-13. The Nicolaitans[10] apparently were a party which converted the liberty of the gospel into license for the flesh. At the time of the Reformation, the tendency found a champion in the person of Johann Agricola. He taught that a man is justified if he believes the promises of the gospel, no matter how impure his life may be. The believer is above the law. He suggested that all who had anything to do with Moses should go to the devil, and that Moses be hanged.[11] Antinomianism is a tendency to be guarded against. Among its several uses, the law also has a didactic function even for the Christian. Torah and nomos, the Old and the New Testament designations for the term "law," are not exactly synonymous, but they do have this in common: that both describe and clarify man's responsibility before God. Torah involves the whole content of the revelation and purpose of God, and thus also emphasizes man's responsibility. Nomos often has the sense of a collection of principles or a legislative code which describes man's responsibility before

10 Rev. 2:6.
11 Wittenberg Disputation, 1537.

God. The moral laws of the Bible are men's interpretation of the will of God in concrete terms, and they must not be ignored or their significance minimized. Paul, long ago, saw that the law is impotent as a way of reconciliation with God, but he still revered the "giving of the law" as a heritage of his race which he cherished[12] along with "the worship, and the promises" that belonged to the Israelites

The Decalogue often has been spoken of as a summary of the law. Such a statement is inadequate; at least until the Decalogue is interpreted in the light and in the spirit of the New Testament. The Decalogue has exerted a tremendous influence upon religious and moral life, but we must not forget how the prophets went beyond the minimal demands of the Decalogue and pleaded for justice and mercy.[13] Justice and mercy are also significant principles for the Christian life. We are not suggesting that the revelation of God has come to man in the form of ideas and codes and principles, but we insist that the revelation of God has, and will, issue in a recognition of moral principles when it is interpreted by man.

The vitality of this position is emphasized when we remind ourselves of the parallels to the legislation of the Decalogue which are to be found outside of the Hebrew tradition. The Code of Hammurabi and the Decalogue do have their similarities, and if we should be disposed to deny historical contacts, the psychological and experiential factors still remain. Historical experience played its part in the formulation of these "principles," and it is to be noted that, in the Book of Exodus, the same chapter states that God wrote the Decalogue and that Moses wrote it.[14] Apparently, to say that God wrote the Ten Commandments and to say that Moses wrote them was to say the same thing. That the

12 Rom. 9:4-5.
13 Hos. 6:6; Amos 5:24.
14 Exod. 34:1, 28.

historical situation had something to do with the giving of the law points to what theology has called "natural law."

Natural Law

Modern theologians have been afraid of the concept of "natural law." They have felt that to recognize the concept would be to place something above God which would challenge his sovereignty. However, natural law is not something determinative for God. It is the regular and constant order by which God rules the universe and which his wisdom presents to the sense and reason of men. The laws of nature and natural instinct, in our modern vocabularies, are not the equivalent of *lex natura*. Natural law is a description of the activity of God in his world. By virtue of its existence, all men can distinguish between right and wrong—and do so, in a greater or lesser degree. Dr. Dodd says, "The implication is that there is in (all men) a capacity for sound moral judgment, a communis sensus which will lead them to recognize as good that which the revealed Law of God declares to be good."[15] The conception of the law of nature finds one of its clearest expressions in Romans 1:19 ff. and 2:14 ff. Anders Nygren deals with this section of Romans in an interesting manner.[16] He tries to make it mean something other than what it says. Karl Barth likewise ignores the implications in these passages. Luther was not averse to recognizing the existence of a natural law. He says, "so we read Moses, not because he concerns us or that we must obey him, but because he rightly corresponds with natural law."[17] Again he says, "I keep the law of Moses, not because Moses

[15] C. H. Dodd, "Natural Law in the Bible," *Theology*, May and June, 1946, p. 6.
[16] Carl C. Rasmussen (trans.), Anders Nygren's *Commentary on Romans* (Philadelphia: Muhlenberg Press, 1949).
[17] *D. Martin Luthers Werke*. Kritische Gesamtausgabe (Weimar, 1883-   ) XXIV, 14. Hereafter referred to as *WA*.

has commanded it, but because it is planted in my nature and Moses rightly corresponds with nature."[18] God's moral order is imprinted in the very nature of our own beings and in the very nature of the universe in which we live. God himself is active in this moral order. Jesus emphasized that an institution like marriage was not due to Jewish law or any special kind of revelation, but was based upon an "order of creation." As male and female, God created man.

Because of modern developments, the phrase "natural law" may have to be discarded. However, there is a truth and an insight involved in this concept which must be revived if our social task is going to be meaningful. Justice is no mere creation of man; it is based upon the holy will of God. Only on the basis of what is involved in the concept of natural law can we find a basis of cooperation for the Christian and the non-Christian. Only on the basis of some such common agreement among men can the Christian speak to the social problems and needs of the world with any degree of hope. Emil Brunner has said that "the opposition to the law of nature has not only prepared the way for the totalitarian state but made it possible."[19] The idea for which this term has stood is necessary and relevant for all time. There may be times when we cannot appeal for a redress of social evils on the basis of the Christian gospel, but we can always make that appeal on the basis of law; and here we often discover a common ground for men of varying theological attitudes, or even agnostics. Robert E. Fitch has said that Charles Darwin was uncertain "about God and immortality" but he recognized "the Moral Law, a universal standard of right and wrong that was built into the structure of nature and of human nature. Like the law of gravitation it was operative everywhere, at all times, among all people. . . . It

18 *WA*, p. 10.
19 Emil Brunner, *Justice and the Social Order* (New York: Harper and Brothers, 1945), pp. 82-89.

was not something abstract and remote; and it could be found in the home. . . . He was sure that he could find it in evolution. When it came to the critical question of what really sets off man from the animals, he recorded his agreement with those writers 'who maintain that of all the differences between man and the lower animals, the moral sense or conscience is by far the most important. . . . It is summed up in that short but imperious *ought,* so full of high significance. It is the most noble of all the attributes of man.' And then he went on to quote Immanuel Kant on the categorical imperative."[20]

When the modern fashion of theology has passed away, it is probable that the valid insights involved in the doctrine of natural law will again find a significant place in theology. The doctrine has been misused in many ways. It has been applied to areas where it has no relevance as, for example, the use Romanists have made of it in connection with their attitude toward birth control. However, the law of God must never be thought of as arbitrary or separate from the nature of creation. There are moral principles which men find and do not make. The nature of the law must be connected with the nature of reality itself or it will lose its relevance. Benjamin Franklin said that "sin is not hurtful because it is forbidden, but it is forbidden because it is hurtful," and so connected the moral law with reality itself. The prophet Jeremiah could say to his people, "Thine own wickedness shall correct thee, . . ."[21] Hosea said to his people, "It is thy destruction, O Israel, that thou art against me, against thy help."[22] In a similar spirit Amos addressed his people, saying, "Seek Jehovah, and ye shall live; . . . Seek good, and not evil, that ye may live; and so Jehovah, the God of hosts,

[20] Robert E. Fitch writing in the *New Republic* (Washington, D. C.), February 9, 1959.
[21] Jer. 2:19.
[22] Hos. 13:9.

will be with you, as ye say."[23] The prophets saw the moral law in the order of creation itself. Sin disintegrates and destroys and a society of none but the wicked would soon destroy itself. The moral law is to be found in the nature of reality itself, and the operation of this law is the activity of God himself in his creation.

The Imitation of Christ

The doctrine of the "imitation of Christ" has fared no better in the hands of some modern theologians than the law. The Christian is called to grow to "the measure of the stature of the fulness of Christ: . . ."[24] The same epistle says, "Be ye . . . imitators of God, . . ."[25] On behalf of God, the Old Testament says to the people of God, ". . . Ye shall therefore be holy, for I am holy"[26] and the New Testament says, "Ye therefore shall be perfect, as your heavenly Father is perfect."[27]

This doctrine, too, has fallen into eclipse in the hands of some modern transcendentalists. The Imago Dei doctrine is related to this matter as it connects man with God as his child, and with Christ as the image of God.[28] It sees in man something more than a brute, or a drop in the vast ocean of nature. This doctrine also sees in man something more than sin. Christianity has never asserted that the essence of human nature is sin. In describing sin, classical dogmatics has always spoken of it as "non essentiale sed accidentale." We must, therefore, distinguish between sin and the sinner. Paul speaks of sin "which dwelleth in me,"[29] and thus makes a

[23] Amos 5:6, 14.
[24] Eph. 4:13.
[25] Eph. 5:1.
[26] Lev. 11:45.
[27] Matt. 5:48.
[28] Col. 1:15.
[29] Rom. 7:20.

clear distinction between sin and the sinner. Furthermore, the doctrine of the sinlessness of Christ would lose all meaning if human nature and sin were to be identified. We must maintain the distinction between Creator and creature, but the doctrine of the Imago Dei still belongs to the Christian tradition. Anders Nygren finds the doctrine difficult to incorporate in his theory. He quotes with approval a statement by E. Lehmann which ascribes the origin of the doctrine to Greek influence, and that is supposed to invalidate it.[30] If we abandon the Imago Dei doctrine, it will be impossible to talk about the "imitation of Christ." Somehow, man's morality and ethics are related to the nature of God. The essence of the moral is a unity for both God and man.

However, as soon as we ask ourselves the question "What do we mean by the imitation of Christ?" we realize that we have a problem on our hands. Jesus lived the life of a celibate; he never assumed the obligations of husband or father. He showed little interest in art, science, or philosophy. The historical Jesus never saw a modern factory and never faced the ethical and moral problems which the modern machine age has created. How, then, can an individual who lived almost two thousand years ago, in faraway Palestine, have anything to say to the twentieth century situation?

Likewise, we are faced with a problem when we look upon the impact of Christianity upon personality in history. The Christian life has unfolded itself in a great variety of forms. There is the hermit, the monk, the crusader, and the social reformer. They all claim to be inspired by Jesus in their particular mode of life and attitude. Furthermore, the Christian life unfolds itself in connection with education, patriotism, economic effort, art, science, and various other fields of interest.

In the midst of all this diversity, what can it mean to imi-

---

[30] Nygren, *Commentary on Romans,* pp. 188-89.

tate Christ or to order our lives in imitation of his life? Underneath all the diversities referred to above we can detect a unique, distinctive quality. There is a sense of the reality of God pressing in upon human life and exerting its influence upon it. Jesus never gave his followers a code of laws as regulative for conduct, and he never outlined any kind of social program. He did give us a spirit which we are to apply to our changing situations. This spirit is applicable to all times, all problems, all conditions. To follow Christ means to translate his spirit into action in our own circumstances. Christian ethics will, therefore, never become obsolete. Christians are called not to an outer imitation of Christ, but to obedience to Jesus' spirit of love. Jesus Christ is our model in disposition, in relation to God and to man. The imitation of Christ offers no ready-made solutions in our ethical decisions, but it does offer us a quality of character in the light of which solutions and a direction are to be found. He who is our Prophet and our Example is also the source of creative power. We would remind ourselves of the words of Luther when he says: "non imitatio facit filios, sed filiatio fecit imitatores."[31]

Legalism

I hasten to add that any norm for Christian social responsibility will not be some form of legalism. Neither a recognition of the significance of law nor an emphasis upon the imitation of Christ need lead to any type of legalism. Legalism has many dangers connected with it. The way of salvation for the legalist is often not by grace, but by law, obedience, and reward. Where grace is allowed to enter, it frequently becomes a concession to human weakness; or it comes as a supplement to man's striving, rather than as some-

[31] *WA*, II, 518.

thing fundamental for all Christian life. The whole idea of merit has to be ruled out for the Christian. Unquestionably, everything that we are or have belongs to God, and there certainly can be no merit in giving God what is already his possession.

The legalist also tends to be bound by a set of detailed and definite rules of conduct. Society is never static and we have no rules by which we can determine a solution for every concrete situation which arises. Love, justice, and mercy are not legalistic rules to be obeyed, but involve a spirit which is always relevant to the social situation. The legalist, in his devotion to the letter of the law, will often violate the very spirit of the law.[32]

The difficulties involved in attempting to use the scripture as a legal code are well illustrated by the difficulties which the church has experienced in dealing with the matter of divorce. The General Council of the Evangelical Lutheran Church in North America took the position that "Violations of the marriage covenant completely disrupting it, are: (a) Adultery, Matt. 5:32; 19:5, 6. (b) Malicious desertion, I Cor. 7:15. While the language of the passages in Matthew seem to restrict divorce to but one ground, 'adultery,' St. Paul in I Cor. 7:15, shows that desertion is the essential principle of adultery."[33] Most of the Lutheran groups in America have, for a considerable period of time, followed this legalistic interpretation and have recognized adultery and malicious desertion as legitimate grounds for divorce. Matthew 5:32 says, "I say to you that everyone who divorces his wife, except on the ground of unchastity, makes her an adultress: and whoever marries a divorced woman commits adultery." Only adultery is recognized in this passage as a

[32] Matt. 23:23.
[33] S. E. Ochsenford, *Documentary History of the General Council of the Evangelical Lutheran Church in North America* (Philadelphia: General Council Publishing House, 1912), p. 391.

legitimate ground for divorce. There are many difficulties involved in the use of this passage as a legitimate ground for divorce. The meaning of fornication and unchastity has to be considered. In the same chapter in which this passage occurs, Jesus says, ". . . I say to you that every one who looks at a woman lustfully has already committed adultery with her in his heart."[34] The question must be asked whether or not that kind of adultery is a legitimate basis for divorce, if the passage in question is to be interpreted in a legalistic sense. It is also to be noted that the exception is not given in the parallel passages in Mark and Luke. In the latter two Gospels, divorce is not legitimatized by Jesus on any grounds. The ideal that there shall be no divorce is emphatically stated. In the light of this circumstance, most modern Bible scholars hold that the exception in Matthew did not belong to the original tradition but was an attempt by the early church to legislate for difficult cases. Furthermore, if the passage in Matthew is a law, it applies only to men. Women are not given the right to divorce their husbands even on the ground of unchastity. Another complication arises when we consider that churches which have recognized adultery as a legitimate ground for divorce have often permitted the remarriage of the innocent party. No such justification can be drawn from this passage. Who or what is going to determine who the innocent party may be? The inconsistencies involved in a legalistic use of Matthew are further revealed when we find that "malicious desertion" has been recognized as a legitimate ground for divorce. In the first place, I Cor. 7:15 does not say that "malicious desertion" is a legitimate ground for divorce and, in the second place, if Matthew recognizes only one ground for divorce we cannot add another from Paul. The impossibility of a legalistic approach to this matter is clear.

[34] Matt. 5:28, R.S.V.

If a legalistic approach to this problem must be rejected, we still must answer the question as to how the church should deal with divorce. The problem well illustrates the nature of the norm of Christian social responsibility.

The ideal emphasized in the New Testament is that marriage should terminate only with death. The Christian ideal is not consonant with divorce on any grounds. Divorce is always a violation of the Christian ideal. Sin is the cause of divorce under any and all circumstances. The church must always hold high the ideal. However, because of sin in the world, divorce does occur. When it does take place, the church must face that sin in exactly the manner it deals with all sin. Here, too, the church must exercise its disciplinary powers, but always in the interest of the temporal and spiritual welfare of all concerned.

Legalism also has sometimes manifested itself in ridiculous forms. On the basis of Mark 9:43 ff., men have been known to cut off their limbs as a means of conquering some form of sin. But the severing of a limb from the body does not remove sin from the soul. On the basis of the words of the apostle Paul, it has been insisted that women wear some kind of covering on the head in the church building.[35] Again, sermons have been preached on the sinfulness of women bobbing their hair.[36] I Timothy 2:11 and 12 have been used as an argument against the propriety of women voting in the assemblies of the church.

We arrive at the same attitude to legalism when we recognize that there are certain social relationships not compatible with the Spirit of Christ, and for which no prohibitions can be found in the Bible. The Bible does not expressly prohibit slavery. Someone has said that the words of emancipation trembled on the lips of Paul when he wrote his letter to

[35] I Cor. 11:5.
[36] I Cor. 11:15.

Philemon on behalf of the runaway slave, Onesimus; but slavery is not expressly prohibited. The Spirit of Christ, however, cannot tolerate any form of slavery. The case relative to war is in the same category. War is not expressly prohibited, but there is something about the spirit of Christianity which is recognized to be incompatible with war, and which makes Christians uncomfortable with the involvements of war. Proof-texts cannot justify either slavery or war, and they will not abolish them. The Bible is not a book of law for the Christian, and moral laws are always subordinate to the spirit of love.

The Sacredness of Personality

Christian social responsibility requires of us that we try to find some fundamental principle which may be used to determine the direction social living ought to take. We need a standard by which to judge social phenomena. We offer no apologetics for this statement, for we have good precedents in the biblical emphasis on law, justice, mercy, and love. We must seek what is essential for a Christian social order. Biblical religion has given us such a principle in its recognition of the sacredness of human personality. This means that, in the realm of social relations, human personality is the highest value we know. The welfare of men and women, boys and girls, is the supreme goal of all social endeavor. Men must never be used as means for other ends but, in the realm of social relations, must always be considered as ends in themselves. Human values are the supreme test in the realm of social living. Human personality is unique. It is sacred in the sense of being set apart. It is sacred in the sense of the original meaning of the word holy. Sin does not alter this fact in any way. This, of course, means that we can speak of the value of human personality, and here again we stand in opposition to Anders Nygren, who will know nothing about the value of man.[37] Jesus did ask his disciples, "Are not ye of much more value than they?"[38] On another occasion, Jesus said, "For what will it profit a man, if he gains the whole world and forfeits his life?"[39] Apparently a human being had some value in the sight of Jesus. We can be sure that the father in the parable of the Prodigal Son valued his son. To imply that God loves what is of no value is a peculiar way of thinking. God is a poor Creator and we reflect on his creative work if what he has created is of no value. The same Bible which speaks about man as a sinner speaks of man as "a little lower than the angels . . ."[40] Man is a sinner, but he is also the crown of God's creation.

Instead of the term "sacredness of personality," we might speak in terms of love for our fellow man; but the former expression is broader than the word "love." To be devoted to the principle of the sacredness of human personality involves love of fellow man, but a sense of social responsibility also includes the patterns and the forms of society and when we deal with this aspect of our subject the word "love" is not applicable. We can hardly speak about loving monogamy as a pattern for marriage. It is true that the fundamental Christian virtue is love, but when we consider our social responsibility we are also interested in the social context in which love functions and therefore the term "sacredness of personality" is to be preferred as a norm for Christian social responsibility. The term points to a social context, to a relative scale of values and describes the meaning of love for the social order.

This norm is not something which we arbitrarily choose. It

[37] Anders Nygren, *Den Kristna Kärlekstanken* (Stockholm: Victor Petersons, 1930), p. 33.
[38] Matt. 6:26.
[39] Matt. 16:26, R.S.V.
[40] Ps. 8:5, A.V.

is given to us by the revelation of God as He has unfolded His nature and purpose in human history. Just to seek to be humane will never prove to be a very significant dynamic in human affairs. The question must be asked as to why we should be humane. It is not primarily our fellow man and his need which call forth our sense of social responsibility, because most of the people about whom we ought to be concerned as Christians we have not even seen. Human personality is sacred to the Christian, not because of anything inherent in man apart from God, but because God has placed such value upon human personality. William Paton stressed this point when he said, "If this humble and obscure man is in reality one whom God has made, whom He made in love, so that he shall never know peace except in loving God in return; if this man is one to whom God speaks; if this man is the object of a divine solicitude so great that the Word became flesh for his salvation, the Son of God died for him —if this be true, then this humble and obscure man has a link with eternity, with the creative love that made the world. He cannot then be rightly treated as a cog in a machine, or as sample of a racial bloodstream, or one of the individual atoms that make up a nation."[41]

This norm was enunciated by the prophets of the Old Testament. They condemned cruelty in wars of conquest, they denounced the cruelties of slavery, they took the part of the oppressed against the privileged classes, and they denounced the evils of child labor. If cheap labor and larger profits are more important than human rights and values, there is no meaning in the condemnation of slavery or of child labor. If the possession of added territory is more important than human rights, condemning wars of conquest and the dispossession of the poor have no meaning. The

[41] William Paton, *The Church and the New Order* (New York: The Macmillan Company, 1941), p. 150.

fundamental principle underlying all the social attitudes of the great prophets calls human rights and welfare primary.

We find the same emphasis in the teaching of Jesus. For him, even the obligations to the sacred ceremonials of religion had to yield before this principle. He defended the action of his disciples when they were accused of violating the law of the Sabbath because they were eating grain which had been plucked on that day. For Jesus, the satisfaction of human need was more important than ceremonial purity.[42] He interpreted the Sabbath commandment in the light of this principle when he said, ". . . The sabbath was made for man, and not man for the sabbath: . . ."[43] From the point of view of our Christian social responsibility, we may apply the words which Jesus spoke about the Sabbath to every area of life. We say that the state was made for man and not man for the state. Industry is made for man and not man for industry. The economic order exists for man and not man for the economic order. Likewise, the farm organization and the labor union exist for man and not man for these organizations. There is a potential social revolution latent in this principle in every area of social life.

The most Christian social order would be a society in which the highest possible development of human personality would be the primary consideration. The Christian may be critical of specific programs and techniques which government may develop as it tries to meet human need, but the enlightened Christian can never speak in derogatory terms of the "welfare" state. Ideally, the whole Christian social outlook is directed toward the welfare of people.

This fundamental principle of Christian social ethics is no idle utopian dream. It is practical, and has been basic—consciously or unconsciously—for every advance that has

42 Mark 2:23.
43 Mark 2:27.

been made down through the history of human civilization.

A denial of this principle was once written into the constitution of one of our states, where we read that, "The right of property is before and higher than any constitutional sanction, and the right of the owner of a slave to such slave and its increase is the same and as inviolable as the right of the owner of any property whatsoever."[44] Few will deny that the emancipation of the slave was an advance in civilization. Under any circumstances it was the Christian thing to do. That emancipation was a recognition of and application of this principle. The person who understands the meaning of the doctrine of the sacredness of personality will see it in operation in the movement to abolish slavery.

Grievous sins have been committed against children. Child labor, by which we understand the work of children under conditions which interfere with their physical, mental and spiritual growth, is being progressively eliminated. As this sordid story in the history of the human race is relegated to history, we see another direct application of the principle of the sacredness of personality.

The emancipation of woman also is due to a recognition of the validity of this principle. In many lands and climes woman is, and has been, a piece of property, owned and disposed of at the will of her husband like any other property. As recently as the twentieth century, the Nineteenth Amendment to the Constitution of our country became law and granted women the franchise. The emancipation of woman from her inferior position is a significant application of the norm of the sacredness of human personality.

Our American public school system is one of the fine things of which we Americans can boast. We today take it as a matter of course, but it was not always so. Governor

---

[44] Kirby Page, *Individualism and Socialism* (New York: Farrar and Rinehart, 1933), p. 36.

Berkely of the colony of Virginia, at the end of the seventeenth century, said, "I thank God we have no free schools or printing; and I hope we shall not have these hundred years. For learning has brought disobedience and heresy and sects into the world; and printing has divulged them and libels against the government. God keep us from both."[45] In connection with the struggles of Horace Mann for popular education, he said, "I believe that this amazing dereliction from duty, especially in our own country, originates more in the false notion which men entertain respecting the nature of their right to property, than in anything else. . . . The rich man who has no children declares that the exaction of a contribution from him to educate the children of his neighbor is an invasion of his rights of property."[46] In this statement by Horace Mann we see the struggle between an application of the principle of the sacredness of personality and property rights. But who will deny that the ascendancy and victory of the application of the principle of the sacredness of personality was a step in the right direction?

In the realm of government, democracy is the closest approach to an application of the principle of the sacredness of personality. Democracy and Christianity are not to be equated, and Christianity has existed where democracy has not been known. However, democracy means that every man has a vote, and equality before the law. Wealth does not vote in a democracy. It is people who vote. Human values are placed above property values, and so again the principle is being applied. There have been trends toward democracy outside the Hebrew-Christian tradition, but I think it can be said, without contradiction, that the most dynamic force in history toward democracy has been that tradition.

[45] *Ibid.*, p. 37.
[46] *Ibid.*, pp. 39-40.

At any rate, the closest approach to an application of our norm to the realm of government is democracy.

Partisan Identification

A word must be spoken against the tendency to find a Christian norm in partisan allegiance. The Christian is involved in politics, and the political realm must not be abandoned by the Christian to the non-Christian. We are concerned that politics be governed by Christian principle and that politicians function as Christians. We are also concerned that every Christian assess his political functions in the light of the Christian ideal. The Christian should not forget his faith when he votes. However, we cannot identify Christianity with any political party or with any pressure group. The Christian, of necessity, will exercise his political functions within the framework of political partisanship, but his primary allegiance is to Christ, not the party.

The church cannot ally itself with any political party but should define its own position on social matters and then let parties assume their attitude to that position. We ought to support or condemn a politician not because he is a member of a certain party, but because of his attitude to what we consider valid for us as Christians. The church can appeal for support for programs and measures only because it considers them to be right and because they are Christian, or more Christian, than other alternatives. Identification of the church with political parties is a dangerous matter. In the first place, there is so much sin in all parties that such identification becomes a denial of the faith. Christ stands in judgment over all political parties. In the second place, parties often change their complexion in the light of historical developments. There was a time Republicans were called "Red Republicans."

The Christian is involved in politics, and he certainly should not remain aloof from the political arena; but the Christian faith, rather than party allegiance, should be the determining factor. In this political realm, also, the principle of the sacredness of personality becomes a significant guide for determining our allegiance. If anyone doubts the vitality of the principle of the sacredness of personality, let him give it a sincere trial in the political realm and he will soon discover its relevance.

5

THE CHURCH
AND SOCIAL RESPONSIBILITY

The Doctrine of the Church

The word "church" has many meanings and is used in many senses—both historically and in the contemporary scene. We use it to designate a particular denomination, such as the United Lutheran Church. It is frequently used to signify the church building at a certain address. Sometimes it stands for a particular corporate congregation as a legal entity.

It is significant for us to note the meaning of the term as it is used in the New Testament. The word translated "church" means "called out," and refers to the assembly of Christians who have been called out from the world. One of the earliest manifestations of the development of a "church" is found in the activity of the prophet Isaiah. He speaks of himself as a teacher, and he had gathered about himself a group of disciples whom he considers to be a gift of God. He instructed them and sent them out to preach and teach.[1] Here was a group of disciples who had a unique position in the nation and were "called out" and separated from the nation for a particular purpose. If not the earliest, it is one of the earliest "churches" in history.

In the New Testament, the word "church" is sometimes used to designate a local situation. Paul uses it in this sense

[1] Isa. 8:16-22.

when he says, ". . . salute the church that is in their house."[2]
He also uses the expression, "to the church in thy house."[3]
Paul also could speak about "the church of the Thessaloni-
ans" in addressing them. Paul calls these local groups of
Christians "the church" and the church in all its essential
fulness was there. The means of grace create the church
when they are received in faith, for the forgiveness of sins
and life in the Spirit.

That there are assemblies of Christians who have been
"called out," scattered throughout the world, is also a fact.
There is a sense in which all Christians constitute the church
and in this sense the word is used in Matthew 16:18. The
church is not a political unit nor an ecclesiastical organization, in the New Testament sense of the word. In this doctrine of the church as well as with respect to sacerdotalism,
Luther completely broke with Rome and the Middle Ages.
For Lutheranism, the church is the communion of saints,
in which the Word of God is taught in its purity and the
sacraments are administered in accordance with the institution of Christ.[4] An empirical organization is necessary, but
it is only by a figure of speech that we can speak of this outward organization as the church.

Luther says that "the Church is called the assembly of all
the believers in Christ upon earth . . . just as we pray in
the Creed: 'I believe in the Holy Ghost, a communion of
saints.' This community or assembly consists of all those
who live in true faith, hope and love; so that the essence,
life and nature of the Church is not a bodily assembly, but
an assembly of hearts in one faith. . . . Thus, though they
be a thousand miles apart in body, yet they are called an
assembly in spirit because each one preaches, believes, hopes,
loves, and lives like the other. . . . That means in reality a

[2] Rom. 16:5.
[3] Philemon 1:2.
[4] Tappert, *op. cit.*, "The Augsburg Confession, Article VII," p. 32.

spiritual unity, because of which men are called a communion of saints. . . . The Church is made separate from all temporal communities, as not being anything external. And this blind Romanist makes it an external community. . . . The Church is not at Rome, nor is it bound to Rome or any other place, but it is where there is faith in the heart. . . . Therefore whoever maintains that an external assembly or an outward unity makes a Church, sets forth arbitrarily what is merely his own opinion. . . . The conclusion is inevitable, that just as being in the Roman unity does not make one a Christian, so being outside of that unity does not make one . . . unchristian. . . . Therefore all those who make the Christian communion a material and outward thing, like other communities, are in reality Jews. . . . A man is not reckoned a member of the Church according to his body, but according to his soul, nay, according to his faith. . . . The Church is a spiritual community, which can be classed with a temporal community as little as spirits with bodies, or faith with temporal possessions. . . . Whosoever would not go astray should, therefore, hold fast to this, that the Church is a spiritual assembly of souls in one faith, and that no one is reckoned a Christian for his body's sake; in order that he may know that the true, real, right, essential Church is a spiritual thing, and not anything external or outward, by whatever name it may be called." The kind of unity of which Luther continues to speak in this connection "is of itself sufficient to make a Church, and without it no unity, be it of place, of time, of person, of work, or of whatever else, makes a Church."[5]

Relation of the Church to the Kingdom of God

In considering the relation of the church to our subject, it is necessary to keep clearly in mind what we mean by the

[5] *PE*, p. 332 ff.

term "church." We must not make of the church what it is not by its nature. The doctrine of the church is important and we would not minimize it, but it is significant that, as far as we know, Jesus used the term only twice.[6] The second of these two passages may reflect an historical background a good deal later than the earthly life of Jesus. There is a theological theory abroad in the world today which would make of the church itself the very essence of Christianity. The church is a part of God's kingdom but *only* a part. The church is also God's instrument through which God is working to accomplish his good will. The church is instrumental to the fulfillment of God's purpose. It is not the goal of that purpose, at least it is not considered so on this side of the parousia.

There are those who claim that Christ and his church are one. Bishop Aulen says, "Christ and the Church belong together. They constitute an inseparable unity. The Church has its existence in and through Christ. But neither does Christ exist apart from his Church."[7] ("Men icke heller Kristus existerar utan sin kyrka.") That this statement is not a word casually spoken is evident from the fact that Aulen quotes from Nygren as being in agreement with him. He quotes the latter as saying, "When the church is designated as the body of Christ and Christ as the head of the church, it does not mean that one part is given to Christ and another to the church, but rather to emphasize their inseparable togetherness and unity. Christ is not simply the head, but precisely the head for his church. And the church is not simply the body, apart from the head, but precisely the body of Christ. The body of Christ is Christ himself. The church is Christ, who after his resurrection is present among us and meets us here on earth."[8] It should be added

[6] Matt. 16:18; 18:17.
[7] Gustaf Aulen, *Den Allmanliga Kristna Tron* (4th ed.; Stockholm: Svenska Kyrkans Diakonistyrelses Bokförlag, 1943), p. 362.
[8] *Ibid.*, p. 362.

that Aulen has modified his position in a later edition of his work, but the earlier edition does exemplify a certain mind-set which is significant.

This atitude amounts to virtually a divinization of the church. It is practically idolatry, because it exalts the relative to the place of the absolute. This is precisely another form of one of the fundamental errors of Catholicism. We are not particularly concerned to assert that Catholicism practices idolatry, but rather that it *is* idolatry in that it makes what is relative, absolute. Paul makes clear distinction between Christ and his people. They are one with him in the work and in the trials to which he has called them, but his people are not identical with him.[9] The church itself stands under judgment and in need of constant renewal and transformation. Furthermore, to make use of the figure of the church as the body of Christ in such a literalistic manner as Aulen and Nygren have done is just poor exegesis. The church is not Christ, but it is his servant.

The Church of Rome

Any student of church history is aware that the Church of Rome has had a certain social consciousness. The ultimate goals of the church may be subject to severe criticism, and the social impact of the Church of Rome in Spain, Portugal, South America, and Poland, not to mention other Roman Catholic countries, leaves much to be desired. However, during the Middle Ages the church did recognize a certain responsibility for the character of society. It did exert an influence upon group life socially, economically, and nationally. The ideal had been a church-state. The pope had tried to control temporal as well as spiritual affairs. Every area of interest for man was part of a larger unity. Education, art,

9 I Cor. 15:23.

and science were all viewed in the light of the theological framework of the church. The church influenced the economic order when it forbade the taking of interest and when it encouraged the development of the guilds for the welfare and protection of the workers.

Social interest on the part of the Church of Rome needs no theoretical justification for Catholics. Two of the best known modern papal encyclicals emphasize this. In 1891, Leo XIII issued his famous encyclical Rerum Novarum, on the condition of Labor. Forty years later, Pius XI issued his encyclical Quadregesimo Anno, on reconstructing the social order, in commemoration of Rerum Novarum. Joseph Husslein, in his systematic interpretation of these two encyclicals, says that his work "presents ... a survey of the social doctrine of the Church as taught by her highest representatives. It is in a sense, a Christian Sociology, as set forth by the Sovereign Pontiffs."[10] The Catholic church in our own country has often manifested an enlightened social consciousness. Pope Benedict XV, in a letter addressed to the Bishop of Bergamo states: "Let no member of the clergy imagine that . . . social activity is outside his priestly ministry on the ground that it lies in the economic sphere. It is precisely in this sphere that the salvation of souls is in peril. Hence, it is Our desire that priests regard it as one of their obligations to devote themselves as far as possible to social theory and action, by study, observation, and work, and that they support in all ways those who in this sphere exercise a wholesome influence for the good of Catholics."[11] Pius XI says, "No easy task is here imposed upon the clergy, wherefor all candidates for the sacred priesthood must be adequately prepared to meet it by intense study of social matters."[12]

[10] Joseph Casper Husslein, *The Christian Social Manifesto* (Milwaukee: Bruce Publishing Company, 1931), p. 328.
[11] *Ibid.*, p. 254.
[12] *Ibid.*, p. 236.

The activities of the National Catholic Welfare Conference in the United States are well known. Note that this conference functions under the direction of the bishops of the church and is no mere addendum to the ecclesiastical machinery. Examples can be given of programs which have been developed which have served the genuine welfare of people.

In 1925, the pope issued an encyclical, Anno Santo, in which he established a new festival for the church year, a festival of Christ, the King. In this encyclical it is stated expressly that the Roman church is the kingdom of God on earth. This was no new doctrine in the Roman church. Very early in the history of the church the idea of "the kingdom" began to be displaced by the idea of "the church." "Augustine completed this process in his De Civitate Dei. The millenium began when the church was founded. This practically substituted the actual, not the Ideal Church for the Kingdom of God. The beloved ideal of Jesus became a vague phrase which kept intruding from the New Testament. Like Cinderella in the kitchen, it saw the other great dogmas furbished up for the ball, but no prince of theology restored it to its rightful place. The Reformation, too, brought no (renascence) of the doctrine of the Kingdom; it had only eschatological value, or was defined in blurred phrases borrowed from the Church."[13] Theology was now concerned "and by its theoretical discussions did its best to stimulate sacramental actions and priestly importance. Thus the religious energy and enthusiasm which might have saved mankind from its great sins, were used up in hearing and endowing masses, or in maintaining competitive church organizations, while mankind is still stuck in the mud. There are nations in which the ethical condition of the masses is the

[13] Walter Rauschenbusch, *A Theology for the Social Gospel* (New York: The Macmillan Company, 1917), pp. 132-33.

odd reverse of the frequency of the masses in the churches."[14]

When the doctrine of the church became a substitute for the doctrine of the kingdom, we witness a fall of Christianity. When the church arrogates to itself and to sinful men the prerogatives that belong to the kingdom of God, we have reached a state of idolatry. The temporal power of the church must not be substituted for the kingdom of God. Furthermore, we are unalterably opposed to the proposition that the church should be established as a temporal power. We insist upon the separation of church and state, from both the point of view of the New Testament and our democratic institutions. We are not willing that an ecclesiastical hierarchy, as such, shall exercise temporal power. To be sure, such separation of church and state is functional, and both of these orders have their origin in God's will and ought to function in accordance with his will. It will always be the function of the church to leaven thought and action for its members for the affairs of the state, and if the church fails at this point the state will become a law unto itself and religion will become irrelevant for the social sphere. However, this is something entirely different than to vest the church with temporal power and make it the administrator of programs. The temporal power of the church during the Middle Ages and in more modern times does not inspire us with any degree of enthusiasm to vest the church with temporal power. Temporal power for the church has usually been an evil, not only in connection with Romanism but, also, wherever it has existed. In emphasizing the social relevance of Christianity, we are not proposing a church-state ideal; nor the situation in Calvin's Geneva experiment, in which he tried to make the invisible sovereignty of God as tangible and visible as the Medieval church had been. We are not advocating the type of sovereignty involved in the

[14] *Ibid.*, p. 134.

various historical attempts to establish theocracies. We are rejecting all attempts to place temporal power in the hands of the church. The church has only one sword and that sword is "the sword of the Spirit, which is the word of God: . . ."[15] Through witnessing to that word the church makes its primary social impact.

The identification of the church and the kingdom appears in Luther, also, and it is not surprising that he was unable to divest himself completely of his medieval background. When, in his Catechism, he interprets the Second Petition of the Lord's Prayer, he certainly does not identify the church with the kingdom; but in his "Answer to the Celebrated Romanist at Leipzig" he makes this mistake. He has spoken of the unity of the church as being not an external unity and then, by way of substantiation, he quotes the words of Christ to Pilate when Christ said, "My kingdom is not of this world." Then Luther adds, "This is indeed a clear passage, in which the Church is made separate from all temporal communities, as not being anything external."[16] That Luther, in this connection, confused the kingdom and the church is evident in that he fails to make a distinction between the two.

Bishop Aulen makes the same mistake. He says, "Just as impossible as it is to think about the church apart from Christ, it is to think about Christ—the Lord—apart from his area of sovereignty, or apart from the communion which belongs to him. Where Christ is, there is the church. The sentence can also be turned around: where the church is, there is Christ. . . . Christ has taken form in his church. . . . The church is, under earthly circumstances, the living and continuously active form for the revelation of Christ."[17] He also says, "The church can be described as the kingdom of

15 Eph. 6:17.
16 *PE*, I, 349.
17 Aulen, *op. cit.*, p. 362.

Christ, regnum Christi, as it exists under earthly conditions."[18] There is also a tendency in Aulen's work to identify the empirical organization with the church.[19] As he looks over this Romanizing precipice, he finds it difficult to maintain his balance and says, "But it means that faith does not lose the insight as to what it is that makes the church a church."[20] I am not disposed to attribute to the "regnum Christi" some of the things that I know from the history of the church.

To make the kingdom synonymous with the church is to make the church what it is not. If we substitute the word "church" wherever "kingdom" occurs in the Gospels, we soon discover it is impossible to identify the church with the kingdom.[21] The situation becomes just as absurd if we substitute the word "kingdom" where the word "church" occurs.[22] The church is important and it is a means (and an indispensable means) by which God advances the goals of the kingdom, but it does not have the central place that the kingdom of God had in the thinking of Jesus. We must not minimize the significance of the church, but we must set our doctrine of the church in the framework of the doctrine of the kingdom. Without the doctrine of the kingdom of God we may have systems of redemption and humanistic ethical systems, but we shall find it difficult to establish any organic relationship between them and the social order.

In a great many treatises on dogmatic theology, the kingdom of God is scarcely mentioned. A cursory look at the indices to the works on systematic theology will reveal this. Often when the phrase is used the author reveals his lack of understanding of the meaning of the kingdom of God. Often

18 *Ibid.*, p. 361.
19 *Ibid.*, p. 367 ff.
20 *Ibid.*, p. 369.
21 *See* Matt. 3.2; Mark 1:15; Matt. 5:3; and Luke 12:32.
22 *See* Matt. 18:17.

the kingdom is identified with the church and this is, perhaps, the most common mistake. Walter Rauschenbusch
enumerates a list of consequences which follow any loss of
emphasis upon the kingdom of God. He says "the church
then moves up into the position of the supreme good. The
conscience of the church is then often muzzled, for the kingdom is the test and corrective of the influence of the church.
Without a consciousness of the kingdom the church may
become a reactionary social force, as it is the kingdom that
contains the revolutionary force of Christianity. Movements
for social justice are left without a religious backing when
the kingdom idea is lost. Secular life is often belittled as
compared with services rendered in and through the church.
The church without the idea of the kingdom tends to breed
priests and theologians while it is the vision of the kingdom
which breeds prophets. Without the kingdom there may be
an emphasis on worship in the church without righteousness."[23]

Even so early in the church's history as the time of formulation of the ecumenical creeds, the kingdom of God was
relegated to a position subordinate to the church's. The
Nicene Creed says of Jesus Christ that his "kingdom shall
have no end." Note the eschatological emphasis in this one
instance where the kingdom is mentioned. The significance
of the kingdom for the social order can be gathered only by
implication. Likewise, most of the hymnals of the church
have had very little to say about the kingdom. The new
Service Book and Hymnal of the Lutheran Church in America has the merit of having one section of hymns devoted to
the kingdom of God, even though it contains only eight
hymns. There are also a number of prayers in this book
which deal with the kingdom and the social concerns of the
Christian and the church. One deserves to be quoted in full

[23] Rauschenbusch, *Theology . . . Social Gospel*, pp. 133 ff.

because it is something rather new in the history of Lutheranism. It reads:

> "O Lord, who hast set before us a great hope that thy kingdom shall come on earth, and hast taught us to pray for its coming: Make us ever ready to thank thee for the signs of its dawning, and to pray and work for the perfect day when thy will shall be done, on earth as it is in heaven; who livest and reignest with the Father and the Holy Ghost, one God, world without end. *Amen*."[24]

The church and the kingdom are not identical concepts or realities. It is the primary function of the church to witness, by Word and by life, to the presence of the kingdom.[25] Even the sacraments, from Luther's point of view, are related to the Word. He says the scripture does not say "A righteous man shall live by the sacraments, but 'by his faith'; for it is not the sacraments, but faith in the sacraments, that gives life and righteousness." He further says that "a man can become righteous by faith without bodily reception of the sacraments, so long as he does not despise them; but without faith no sacrament is of any use, nay, it is altogether deadly and pernicious. . . . Now, as we plainly see, God deals with us in no other way than by His holy Word and the sacraments, which are like signs or seals of His Word."[26] For Luther, the Word was central, even in the worship service of the church. He says, "The principal part is to preach and teach God's Word." The fundamental task of the church is to witness through the Word to the world. And even the sacraments are like signs and seals of this Word. As a witness, the church will become the "salt of the earth" and the "light of the world."[27] However, it must bear witness to something

---

[24] *Service Book and Hymnal* (Minneapolis, etc.: Augsburg Publishing House, etc., 1958), p. 227.
[25] Acts 1:8. [26] *PE*, III, 19 ff.
[27] Matt. 5:13, 14.

beyond itself. We cannot measure the success of the church in terms of membership statistics. The kingdom imposes on the church a task of social responsibility, and if the church fails to witness to the state, with respect to its ethics and morals, who shall perform the task? The mission of the church is to witness to the Word of God, and wherever and whenever moral issues are at stake it must speak even to the state. The church has the Word, and this Word is relevant to the affairs of that "order of creation" which we designate the state.

Relation of Church and State

That matters of state are definitely matters which concern the church, has been abundantly demonstrated in our generation. The rise of various forms of fascism and communism in the modern world have impressed upon the church the fact that it cannot ignore the form the state assumes. Both of these movements are secular forms of religion. They demand wholehearted obedience to authority. They offer a gospel of salvation for the individual and for society; they worship their heroes as Saviors; they have their authoritative writings, dogmas, and some measure of cult; they elicit devotion and self-sacrifice; there is an intense partisanship and missionary zeal; there are martyrs, holy wars, and vivid apocalyptic hopes. These are the marks of religions which seek the allegiance of mankind. They are ways of life; and unless the Christian faith meets them with its faith as a way of life, the challenge will not be met at all. People are asking what relevancy the Christian faith has for life, and unless we give an answer the church will be ignored.

As we look at history we find four different relationships manifested with respect to the relation of the church to the state. The state, at times, has been hostile to the church.

Before the days of Constantine, the state often persecuted the church; and this has also been true at other times as well as in modern times. At other times, the state has dominated the church. The Old Byzantine Empire, czarist Russia, and some Protestant countries of Europe are examples. The absurdity of this relationship is illustrated by the principle *cuius regio eius religio,* under which the inhabitants of the Rhenish Palatinate had to change their religion four times in sixty years. Vital religion cannot flourish where people are forced to adopt the religion of the monarch.

A third relationship has existed under which the church has dominated the state. This has been an ideal striven for by the Church of Rome, and at times it has been attained. We have already rejected this attitude as an ideal to be striven for. A fourth relationship has maintained the separation and independence of church and state. This is the ideal for which the constitution of our land stands, and which was inherent in the principles of the Reformation of the sixteenth century.

The words of Jesus, ". . . Render therefore unto Caesar the things that are Caesar's; and unto God the things that are God's,"[28] have often been quoted as a proof-text in support of the doctrine of the separation of church and state. The passage does imply the existence of two separate realms, but it has often been forced to carry more meaning than it did on the lips of Jesus.

At the time of Jesus there were at least three attitudes to Rome on the part of Jews. One party was revolutionary and ready to raise the banner of revolt if favorable circumstances presented themselves. A second party was complacent and well satisfied with the situation as it was. A third group felt uncomfortable under Roman domination, but chose peace by submission. Jesus took the part of the third group,

28 Matt. 22:21.

and what he meant by the statement quoted above was that the Jews should pay their taxes to Caesar as long as God could be worshiped and served by them. Jesus realized that revolution against Rome would be fatal and futile. He also realized that because Jerusalem would not consider "the things that make for peace," but would keep on looking for a chance to revolt, it would be destroyed.[29] Jesus never said —and never implied—that the church has nothing to do with the social order or with the state. Such an implication cannot be drawn from his words, in the interest of a quietistic type of piety.

The state is a political unit. It is the political unit which makes and enforces law. As we have defined the church above, in its true essence the church is not a political unit. If these definitions of the church and state are maintained, church and state are separate by their very nature. On the basis of these definitions, we say not only that church and state ought to be separate, we say they *are* separate. There are two different realms: the one church, the other state. The state and the church have two different functions and these functions must not be confused. The doctrine of the separation of church and state is based upon a recognition of separate functions for church and state.

This does not mean the church is not concerned with the problems of society or the state. Members of the church function in the state, and it is incumbent upon them to strive to function, in this capacity, as Christians. Furthermore, the church must interpret the will of God to the state. The church has an obligation, in the name of God, to speak to the state, for the state is also God's order. In addition, it is the duty of the church to enlighten the conscience of its membership so the will of God may be accomplished in the social realm. There are two realms, and church and state have

29 Luke 19:41-42, R.S.V.

separate functions, but these realms are not parallel lines which never meet. They constantly cross each other and, while it is the province of the state to wield temporal power, it is the province of the church to speak to the state, in the name of God, with respect to his will.

We are not interested in developing a theocracy, in gaining temporal power for the church, in permitting the state to use the church as a tool, or in having the church function as a political unit. We are concerned that the church act as a leaven for human thought and action so the spirit of the Christian faith may permeate the social order. When we speak of Christianizing the state, we do not mean writing the name of God or Christ into the constitution of the land. What we do want is an incorporation of the spirit of our faith in our laws, in our political life, and in our social programs. We want to apply the norm of the last lecture in all the various relationships of life, individually and socially. This is the meaning of Christian social responsibility.

Class Structure and the Church

If the church is to bear the kind of witness suggested above, it will mean broadening the meaning of the term "evangelism." Evangelism will not be simply a preaching mission on a revivalistic note. Christians must be made to understand that evangelism involves the impact of Christian ideas and ideals on every aspect of man's daily living. The labor union or the farm organization may be the stage for an effective evangelism in the measure in which Christian ideals are presented and put into action. If this is to be done, it will be imperative for the church to be cognizant of, and sympathetic to, the needs of all classes of men. It is at this point that preaching and teaching must be made relevant, if they are to have an appeal to man.

One of the great problems which the church faces, in this connection, is one which goes way back to the beginnings of the industrial era. It is a problem particularly for the Protestant church. The church has tended to be dominated by a bourgeois psychology, and this has alienated—to a large extent—whole classes of people.

This problem is not confined to America; it is discovered on the continent of Europe and in the Scandinavian countries. In one of Europe's theological schools, a survey recently was made of the occupational backgrounds of the students' families. Of the 344 questioned, only nine came from industrial workers' families. Eleven came from farms, 120 from employers' or managers' families, and 103 came from families of a professional nature. In another school it was found that out of a group of 173 students, only two came from homes where the father was an industrial worker and only five came from farms. If the overwhelming number of leaders in the church come from the bourgeois segment of society, it is a very serious matter and should lead to earnest self-examination on the part of the church. Various movements of a Christian character in postwar Germany indicate how keenly some of the leadership in the church feels this problem. I refer to such movements as the Kirchentag, the Evangelical Academy, and the "Evangelische Männerarbeit der Evangelischen Kirche in Deutschland."

In America we do not like to talk about classes in society, but the fact remains that they do exist. Sociologists recognize three classes, with various subdivisions. The upper class involves about three per cent of the population, the middle class includes about forty per cent, and the lower class about fifty-seven per cent.[30] It is not difficult to determine which class is dominant in the church when we notice the locations

---

[30] Joseph Alan Kahl, *The American Class Structure* (New York: Rinehart and Company, Inc., 1957).

which our Protestant churches choose when they move from the inner city areas. As far back as 1884 the *Andover Review* stated that it is "by no means altogether a result of evil that the churches stand for what is respectable and even refined, nor within proper limits, that certain lines of social cleavage appear in the group of people in denominations and in the several churches. Let the fact be recognized, then, that as the church has the better classes of society, it will be disliked by the worse classes who are yet outside."[31]

Kahl, in his study of the class structure of our country, says, "Even churches—institutions supposedly rejoicing in the common brotherhood of a common Father, are class typed. In most American towns the people of higher status belong to those Protestant denominations that feature services of quiet dignity and restrained emotion . . . The common men are more often seen . . . where the services are more vigorous, or in Catholic churches, (reflecting their origins from southern or eastern Europe). Those lower-class individuals who go to church at all are most likely to join revivalistic and fundamentalist sects. Some authors believe that the higher status groups are expressing, in ritual and dogma, attitudes of conformity and support for the good life within the current social system; whereas the religions of the lower status people are offering a palliative for failure in this life through salvation in the next."[32]

Class distinctions have reference to a cultural type. Class is, among other things, a matter of psychology and a sense of belonging. The middle class, which is so characteristic of large sections of the church, has an easily recognizable set of attitudes. The middle-class person usually lives in a suburb, in a home which he owns, though there may be a mortgage on the house. His pleasures usually revolve around material

[31] Henry Farnham May, *Protestant Churches and Industrial America* (New York: Harper and Brothers, 1949), pp. 120-21.
[32] *Ibid.*, pp. 149-50.

things and comforts. He has a certain sense of security and tries to provide for his retirement and the education of his children. He is individualistic in his economic theories. He hates bureaucracy and regimentation. Social welfare must never be allowed to restrict his economic theories and liberties. He believes that laissez faire made America great. He is suspicious of, and sometimes negative, in his attitude to labor unions. Labor leaders and their motives are suspect. He believes in honesty, thrift, efficiency, and hard work. He is usually affiliated with a church; and even though the faith of the church does not affect him very seriously, he believes in insurance even if he should never cash in on it. In business relationships, he is hardheaded but usually willing to contribute to charitable and community causes. He believes in his class and is confident that it is the depository of the national ideal. In the measure that his Christian faith touches his economic theories, it issues in an emphasis upon stewardship, vocation, and charity. However, the social patterns in which those virtues are to manifest themselves give him very little concern. Reflecting this view of life, his political theories tend to be conservative as he seeks to maintain the status quo in the situation and environment of which he is a part.

Middle-class people may be so isolated from the underprivileged groups of society that they fail to understand the problems and the needs of these groups, and therefore lack a sense of social responsibility to them. It should be pointed out, also, that general denominational statistics do not reveal the class structure of the church, because it is on the level of the individual church that the stratification appears most clearly. If the church is to take its social responsibility seriously, it will be up to the local congregation to create an atmosphere where all classes feel welcome and at home. The laboring man has often been alienated—from the church and the formal expression of the Christian faith in the church—because the church has lost touch with and lacks sympathetic understanding of his problems.

A Social Creed

Throughout its existence, the Federal Council of the Churches of Christ in America manifested a great deal of interest in the social aspects of the Christian faith. Early in the century, a social creed was adopted; and it was revised from time to time as new social problems developed. With few exceptions the social creed confines itself to the enunciation of principles. It is a remarkable document and indicates clearly what a Christian social order implies. This creed is still a significant expression of a sense of social responsibility.

It says the churches should stand for:

1. Practical application of the Christian principle of social well-being to the acquisition and use of wealth; subordination of speculation and the profit motive to the creative and cooperative spirit.

2. Social planning and control of the credit and monetary systems and the economic processes for the common good.

3. The right of all to the opportunity of self-maintenance; a wider and fairer distribution of wealth; a living wage, as a minimum, and above this a just share for the worker in the product of industry and agriculture.

4. Safeguarding of all workers, urban and rural, against harmful conditions of labor and occupational injury and disease.

5. Social insurance against sickness, accident, want in old age, and unemployment.

6. Reduction of hours of labor as the general productivity of industry increases; release from employment at least one day in seven, with a shorter working week in prospect.

7. Such special regulation of the conditions of work of women as shall safeguard their welfare and that of the family and the community.

8. The right of employes and employers alike to organize for collective bargaining and social action; protection of both in the exercise of this right; the obligation of both to work for the public good; encouragement of co-operatives and other organizations among farmers and other groups.

9. Abolition of child labor; adequate provision for the protection, education, spiritual nurture, and wholesome recreation of every child.

10. Protection of the family by the single standard of purity; educational preparation for marriage, home-making, and parenthood.

11. Economic justice for the farmer in legislation, financing of agriculture, transportation, and the price of farm products as compared with the cost of machinery and other commodities which he must buy.

12. Extension of the primary cultural opportunities and social services now enjoyed by the urban populations, to the farm family.

13. Protection of the individual and society from the social, economic, and moral waste of any traffic in intoxicants and habit-forming drugs.

14. Application of the Christian principle of redemption to treatment of offenders; reform of penal and correctional methods and institutions, and criminal court procedure.

15. Justice, opportunity, and equal rights for all; mutual good will and cooperation among racial, economic, and religious groups.

16. Repudiation of war, drastic reduction of armaments, participation in international agencies for the peaceable settlement of all controversies; the building of a co-operative world order.

17. Recognition and maintenance of the rights and responsibilities of free speech, free assembly, and a free press; the encouragement of free communication of mind with mind as essential to the discovery of truth.[33]

This consensus on the social responsibility of the church is one of the most significant documents on the subject in the history of the American church; and it is still, after almost three decades, a vital guide for social action. Note that this creed advocated, in principle, many of the goals which have been realized through legislation, and advocated them long before legislation was enacted. A practical course on social ethics might be given with this creed as an outline. The creed illustrates what it means to apply Christianity to the social order. It points to the kind of a world which would be possible if the Christian faith were seriously applied to the problems of society.

[33] Herman C. Weber (ed.), *Yearbook of American Churches,* "A Record of Religious Activities in the United States for the Year 1932," Issued under the auspices of the Federal Council of the Churches of Christ in America (1933 ed., Los Altos, California: Round Table Press, Inc., 1916-   ), pp. 319-20.

Type used in this book

Body, 11 on 13 Baskerville

Display, Baskerville

Paper

R.R.R. Standard White Antique